Inspection, Inspection, Inspection!

Inspection, Inspection, Inspection!

How OfSTED Crushes Independent Schools and Independent Teachers

Anastasia de Waal

Civitas: Institute for the Study of Civil Society
London
Registered Charity No. 1085494

First Published July 2006

77 Great Peter Street
London SW1P 2EZ

Civitas is a registered charity (no. 1085494)
and a company limited by guarantee, registered in
England and Wales (no. 04023541)

email: books@civitas.org.uk

ISBN (10) 1-903386-51-9
ISBN (13) 978-1-903386-51-4

Typeset by
Civitas and typetechnique

Printed in Great Britain by
Hartington Litho Ltd
Lancing, Sussex

Contents

Author

After a childhood spent in Greece, Albania and Cambridge, Anastasia de Waal studied sociology at the London School of Economics. With a view to going into research on education, she did a PGCE specialising in inner city primary school teaching, going on to teach in an East End London borough for a year. She returned to the LSE the following year where she did an MSc in sociology, joining Civitas in 2004 as a researcher. Anastasia is now Head of Family and Education at Civitas.

Author's Note: A climate of fear

The climate of fear surrounding OfSTED encountered during the research for this report was very striking. A fear of OfSTED's very public and punitive reporting has cowed its fiercest critics and allowed a highly flawed and dysfunctional system of inspection to survive.

The vast majority of those interviewees directly involved in education were unwilling to talk openly about their views on the inspection process and be named. Teachers from both the state and private sector were concerned about the ramifications of criticism of OfSTED. More alarming, however, was the reluctance on the part of teaching unions, independent school umbrella bodies and even members of the Education and Skills Select Committee to talk freely about the inspection process. In several instances, interviewees who *had* initially agreed to be quoted asked to withdraw their comments: yet not, crucially, because they no longer stood by them. As a result, many respondents' identities have had to be disguised.

Executive Summary

- **OfSTED is a lapdog not a watchdog.** OfSTED is not an education watchdog but a government lapdog. It forces schools to comply with the latest and ever-changing fads from Whitehall. It fails to scrutinise or criticise government policy sufficiently.

- **OfSTED has facilitated a government stranglehold**. 'Education, education, education' has been realised as 'inspection, inspection, inspection'. Rather than educational excellence, Blair has achieved educational autocracy, and OfSTED has been intrinsic to this. The government has been able to take control over the minutiae in schools through the force of the inspectorate.

- **OfSTED is enforcing a New Labour monopoly.** OfSTED has a monopoly over quality control in education. The inspectorate's incestuous relationship with the government therefore allows what counts as quality in education to be defined by the whims of the Department for Education. The government has seized control of state schools, telling teachers that there is only one way to teach. Methods and materials which do not fit in with the monopoly are dismissed.

- **OfSTED is sabotaging independent school freedoms.** Since 2003 private schools have been subject to heavy government regulation. It is now impossible to exist as a private school without emulating many state school practices. The regulations for private schools focus not on basic health and safety but on how and what schools teach. The effect is to impose the flaws in the state sector on the private sector.

- **OfSTED is thwarting learning.** The inspectorate is hindering progress and excellence by enforcing time-consuming distractions from frontline teaching. Extensive and pointless paperwork requirements and a focus on artificial targets mean that pupils' learning is becoming a secondary consideration.

- **OfSTED is failing the nation.** OfSTED's stamp of approval does not safeguard parents and children from bad schools. OfSTED does not rate schools according to the quality of education provided; it judges them on how their provision fulfils the government's tick-boxes. On this basis OfSTED fails good schools in the private sector and hinders progress in struggling state schools.

- **OfSTED is arresting parental choice.** The government's talk of parental power and choice is empty rhetoric under the current inspection regime. OfSTED's judgements defy parent power and inspection frameworks thwart choice. Parents who have deliberately opted out of the state system for independent schools now find themselves unable to get away from state-approved pedagogy.

- **OfSTED intimidates schools into compliance**. Fear in both state and private sectors stops schools from resisting government diktat. The repercussions for schools and teachers of straying from central commands are sufficiently damaging that compliance is ensured despite widespread objections.

- **OfSTED is fostering fabrication**. OfSTED's fixation on tick-box procedure has led schools to resort to fabricating the necessary evidence for inspection. OfSTED is interested only in fulfilment of rigid criteria, regardless of how they have been achieved.

- **OfSTED degrades teachers**. Under the current education regime, teachers are automatons, not professionals. The criteria for a good inspection report push aside talent, innovation and good outcomes in favour of standardised procedure.

The objections which are urged with reason against State education, do not apply to the enforcement of education by the State, but to the State's taking upon itself to direct that education: which is a totally different thing. That the whole or any large part of the education of the people should be in State hands, I go as far as any one in deprecating… A general State education is a mere contrivance for moulding people to be exactly like one another… in proportion as it is efficient and successful, it establishes a despotism over the mind, leading by natural tendency to one over the body. An education established and controlled by the State, should only exist, if it exist at all, as one among many competing experiments, carried on for the purpose of example and stimulus, to keep the others up to a certain standard of excellence.

John Stuart Mill, On Liberty, 1869

Introduction

In 2004 a small independent school, Charterhouse Square School, caught the attention of the press. It appeared to pose a paradox. Despite outstanding results in the government's very own tests (SATs), an exemplary record of feeding pupils into top secondary schools, and a perennial waiting list, OfSTED had given Charterhouse Square School a damning inspection report. While 'market' measures defined Charterhouse Square School as a very good school, the government's education watchdog found it to be providing a substandard education. If Charterhouse Square School failed to address the weaknesses OfSTED had identified—with an extensive number of changes and implementations—it would face closure.[1]

> ***For some reforms, at some times, it has been necessary and right to take a fierce grip, deliver dramatic change quickly, to make right a problem in the system. We will never apologise for the directive action we took, for example, on literacy and numeracy…***
>
> *DfES: Five Year Strategy for Children and Learners, 2004*

To many, the surprise was more than just the discrepancy between the school's academic record and the inspectorate's judgement. Rather it lay in the discovery that OfSTED inspected the private sector at all, and moreover seemed to have accrued considerable powers over how independent schools ran themselves. OfSTED was not simply inspecting basic issues relating to health and safety in the private sector, it was making judgements on how and what schools taught.

Charterhouse Square School's paradoxical inspection ruling was by no means unique. Further investigation found that many other similarly successful private primary schools had been poorly graded.

OfSTED's reporting on the private sector sparked several fundamental questions. How did OfSTED come to have so much power over independent schools? Why was the inspectorate finding ostensibly successful schools to be providing an unsatisfactory education? What impact was OfSTED inspection having on independent provision?

The apparent penalising of the private sector may seem of limited relevance to the education debate in light of the current crisis in state schools. The number of pupils educated in the private sector is very small—around just seven per cent of the school-aged population.[2] Furthermore, the number of schools inspected directly by OfSTED—like Charterhouse Square School—is even smaller, around three per cent of the school-aged population.[3] This is because what are termed 'association' schools, those whose heads are members of associations in the Independent Schools Council (ISC), are inspected by their own, (albeit OfSTED monitored) inspectorate, the Independent Schools Inspectorate (ISI). Yet although the main objects of the report are few in number, the principle of OfSTED's intervention in the independent sector is an indictment of the education sector as a whole. The inspectorate's activity in private schools is a worrying symptom of New Labour's educational reforms and it raises serious concerns about OfSTED's role in them.

> ***Independent schools must meet the requirements of detailed regulations in order to retain their registration. These schools' ability to meet the regulations must be reported in detail to the regulatory authority.***
>
> *OfSTED: Inspection of non-association independent schools, 2005*

Investigation into OfSTED's judgements of independent schools revealed that schools frequently received unfavourable reports, not due to poor basic provision, but because they did not conform to the prescriptive pedagogies espoused by the government. Despite their nominal independence from central authority, private schools are now bound by law to comply with a fastidious set of regulations dictated by the government: 'in exercise of the powers conferred on the Secretary of State by sections 157(1) and 210(7) of the Education Act 2002(1)'.[4] These regulations range from basic health and safety requirements to detailed teaching and learning stipulations. OfSTED's role in the private sector is to ascertain, and where necessary enforce, schools' compliance with these. Crucially, as we have seen with the example of Charterhouse Square School, both the regulations themselves and the fulfilment criteria are tightly defined: this is what has generated such anomalous inspection judgements. Critically, these regulations are not only extensive, they are determined, not by an impartial education watchdog, but by the government. Ultimately, what these curbed freedoms of the private sector signify is the problematic combination of a non-independent national inspectorate—OfSTED—with the politicisation of New Labour's education policy.

Well-intentioned education reforms under New Labour have soured in the carrying-out. New Labour's approach to school improvement was flawed from the start and, in light of the financial and time constraints that the government initially set itself, the aim itself was over-zealous. Whilst the indisputably positive goal of higher standards still stands in New Labour's education policies, the government's political agenda has made for systemic distortions. Education has shifted from being central to this government's political agenda to becoming dangerously politicised itself. The nature of the higher standards the government pursues has therefore become questionable.

The government has created a monopoly over what counts as quality in schools, once affecting only the state sector, but now also the private sector. This monopoly has been both caused and driven by the eradication of school autonomy in the state sector. Partnership with the government on the part of the ostensibly neutral OfSTED has been fundamental to the central capturing of what pedagogy is acceptable. There are two strands to OfSTED's intervention in the private sector relating to this pedagogical cartel. Firstly, the extension of government power into the private sector, via OfSTED, has been a natural progression now that state school provision has been 'centralised'. Secondly, OfSTED's assertion of a single optimum model of provision is necessarily undermined by alternatives which produce successful outcomes—as in the private sector.[5]

The Blair government has been unashamed in expressing its desire for the independent sector to become the casualty of a transformed excellent state sector. However this is a different aspiration from 'old' Labour visions of egalitarianism. The aim for New Labour has been less about the vilifying and disposing of an 'elitist' sector and more about undermining the very existence of an 'alternative' sector with the superior quality of state provision. Although class is central to it, Blair initially approached the private/state school divide as a battle over quality rather than class. Blairites talked of an educational 'apartheid' between private and state schools, but their focus was on penetrating this from the state, not the private sector. Unlike those amongst the ranks of old Labour, initiatives such as the City Academies programme, and now Trust schools, demonstrate that Blair does not have a problem with private sector money in education. Virtually 80 per cent of all secondary schools are now city academies, city technology colleges or specialist schools—meaning that virtually 80 per cent of all secondaries receive private investment.[6] These initiatives also show that he does not have a problem with extending management freedoms away from central control, relating to assets and even staffing.[7] But even this independence tends to be ring-fenced:[8] what Blair has proved he does have a problem with is autonomy from government diktat over the principles of education. This helps explain why the prime minister has embraced private involvement in education but was prepared to abolish the Assisted Places scheme.[9] Whilst old Labour saw educational pluralism—in terms of providers—as the enemy of democracy,[10] *pedagogic* pluralism has become the enemy of Blair's reform strategy. For all his talk of choice, Blair has proved that he is not interested in an education market.

Blair's approach to school reforms has centred on government control over the classroom and independent schools and independent teachers threaten this. In this sense former OfSTED Chief Inspector Chris Woodhead is wrong in his assertion that it is not the government or OfSTED but the old Labour backbenchers and members of the Education and Skills Select Committee who have pushed through legislation upping central control over the private sector.[11] (This point is supported by the fact that two key members of the Education and Skills Select Committee were actually *unaware* of the level of scrutiny that private schools are subject to.)[12] The hostility towards the private sector to which Woodhead refers certainly exists in a faction of the Labour party, but it is not so much this which is responsible for government intervention into the private sector. Although Woodhead is also right that Blair 'does not suffer from the ideological hang-ups [towards the private sector] that afflict so many of his backbenchers',[13] he chooses to ignore Blair's 'managerialist' aspirations—inherited not from the egalitarians, but the Conservatives.

> ***The dramatic turnaround in Labour education policy can be clearly identified with Blair himself.***
>
> *Professor Alan Smithers, 2001*[14]

The expansion of the government's reach and subsequently that of OfSTED into the independent sector is symptomatic of the flaws (initial and then redemptive) in the New Labour education project—a project which has been Blair's baby from the start. Whilst education policy has always reflected the political standpoint of the party in power, never before has it been quite so heavily implicated in the Prime Minister's personal agenda. Over the last nine years it is Blair himself who has presided (in presidential manner) over education reforms, his education secretaries often acting more as strategic aides than strategic advisers. With the exception perhaps of Estelle Morris, who resigned after a year modestly claiming not to be 'up to the job',[15] Blair's education secretaries to date have served as loyal Blairites and ensured the general compliance of the potentially uncooperative DfES. It seems likely that at least for the remainder of Blair's premiership, Alan Johnson will be equally accommodating of the improvement drive.

However, it is Blair's tight circle of unelected education 'gurus', the most notable being Andrew (now Lord) Adonis, who arguably have stood most firmly with Blair at the helm of his improvement drive.

Secretaries of State for Education
David Blunkett 1997 – 2001
Estelle Morris 2001 – 2002
Charles Clarke 2002 – 2004
Ruth Kelly 2004 – 2006
Alan Johnson 2006 – present

Chief Inspectors
Stewart Sutherland: 1992 - 1994
Chris Woodhead: 1994 – 2000
Mike Tomlinson: 2000 – 2002
David Bell: 2002 – 2005
Maurice Smith: 2005 – 2006
Christine Gilbert: October 2006 –

Let Blair be his own education chief.
Andrew Adonis, 1996[16]

Lord Adonis, famously nicknamed by educationalist Ted Wragg as 'Tony Zoffis' (i.e. Tony's office)[17] because of his close relationship with the prime minister, has undoubtedly played a significant role in bolstering Blair's autocratic approach to school reform. It was not a coincidence that the prime minister's right hand man in education wrote an article in 1996 arguing that for Blair to carry out his envisaged transformation of the education system Blair should be his own education secretary; 'sustained prime ministerial attention [on education]', argued Adonis, 'is now so necessary'.[18]

Tony Blair came into office with a clear goal of making educational history, personally and within the constraints of his terms: quantifiable progress with rapid effect, and comparatively modest investment. In schools the strategy was to dictate what was taught, when it was taught and how it was taught. Having pledged to stay within the Conservatives' public spending plans for the first two years, there was in fact little else that could be done to transform the system *other* than control it. Thus in New Labour's first two years a flood of new initiatives was accompanied, not by additional money, but additional direction. While the number of press releases issued by the Department for Education went up by more than 50 per cent in New Labour's first year,[19] class sizes swelled and expenditure on education sank lower than under Thatcher.[20] Although investment in education began to rise steadily from 1999, it was by then quite clear that in the primary sector, the government's reform strategy centred on central intervention rather than on investment to improve conditions in schools. As the then Liberal Democrat spokesman for education, Phil Willis, observed about Blair's education policies in 2003: 'They [the government] believe that unless teachers are being told what to do, and then checked to ensure that they are doing it, children's education will suffer'.[21] Yet the controlling approach was flawed as it straitjacketed schools, in many respects worsening rather than improving teaching and learning conditions.

Primary schools, where the government has concentrated its attention, have borne the brunt of the improvement drive, subjected to particularly rigid central dictation in the form of a constant influx of new imitiatives. New Labour's first white paper on education in 1997 set out the reforms that spawned the dictation which has come to shackle the primary sector. These included: the prioritisation of literacy, numeracy and ICT; more testing; more targets; an introduction of annual league tables and an increase in inspections.[22] Over-zealous initiatives loudly trumpeted (and, rather more quietly, often discarded) have done less to improve learning than we have been led to believe. Whilst standards, at least quantifiable ones, have undeniably risen, the improvement has not been at a rate equal to the rhetoric. The introduction of the National Numeracy and Literacy Strategies in primary schools, which involved an unprecedented level of prescription, have not led to the predicted improvement, even according to the government's own questionable measures. In 2005 only 57 per cent of pupils leaving primary school had achieved the expected standard in both English and maths;[23] one in four children currently leave primary school unable to read and write at the level required by the government for their age.[24] According to independent measures, such as those of Durham University's Centre for Evaluation and Monitoring,[25] or most recently Michael Shayer's Piagetian measures of cognitive development,[26] many aspects of primary-aged learning are at a low ebb. Despite the Blairite revolution, the nation's pupils continue to lag embarrassingly behind in comparison with other rich nations. Standards have at best risen only slightly during New Labour's time in power and at worst actually declined in some areas. While the Blair education strategy has certainly created an immense amount of activity in schools, the harm done by such incessant activity, to teacher retention rates for example, has severely undermined much of the progress made.

Over-regulation of schools has been both the central and fatal element of recent education reforms. It is via OfSTED that the government has been able to obtain this damaging control. Set up in 1992 by the Conservatives under Major, OfSTED was most famously headed by its second chief inspector, Chris Woodhead, who pioneered the witch-hunt approach to school improvement. Although Woodhead was both inherently conservative in his views on schooling as well as loathed by the teaching community, Blair was keen to keep him on. Considering the hold over schools Woodhead's draconian approach achieved, it is easy to see why Blair wanted his partnership; and indeed, like-minded views on the importance of literacy and numeracy as well as on commandeering teachers would make them a very powerful duo. A strong relationship between the prime minister and OfSTED was forged which would continue long after Woodhead's departure in 2000.

Subsequent Chief Inspectors may have been less aggressive but OfSTED has never shaken off the punitive image gained under Woodhead. Blair's reform process has coupled OfSTED's coercing power with evangelical rhetoric—in the 1997 education white paper the improvement drive is actually referred to as a *crusade*—to dictate the minutiae in schools. Indeed 'in keeping with its importance to Blair, OfSTED acquired further rights to inspect…'[27] OfSTED's influence in schools and in the public domain means that the inspectorate holds the potential to 'neutrally' determine the direction of provision. The two sources of the inspectorate's power are contradictory: namely, its nominal impartiality and its relationship with the government. OfSTED's independence and objectivity are what lend its inspections and reports credibility amongst 'consumers' of education (i.e. parents) and therefore its dominance in schools. It is the conflicting nature of these two sources of power, its perceived objectivity and its actual lack of independence from the government, which has enabled the government to tightly control education, with the appearance of legitimacy rather than authoritarianism.

Since its establishment OfSTED has been heavily criticised by the educational community. Similarly, criticism of New Labour's education policy is a favourite pastime of both opposition parties. However, little critical attention has been paid to the relationship between the two. OfSTED's susceptibility to political influence has allowed New Labour to take unprecedented control over schools, in both sectors. Both the Conservatives and the Liberal Democrats have failed to make sufficient connection between government policy and OfSTED, particularly surprising on the part of the Conservatives, considering that they paved the way for this relationship. This oversight is extremely important as ultimately it is OfSTED which is enforcing the implementation of these criticised policies in schools. Yet rather than attacking OfSTED's mechanisms, the opposition parties confusedly use OfSTED's judgements to support their assaults on education standards. OfSTED evidence is treated as the evidence of an independent watchdog, rather than that of a government lapdog.

The only hope of salvaging our struggling maintained schools from their current state of agitated stagnation is to free them from the government's strangulating control. What we are witnessing with the government's intervention in the private sector is a microcosmic illustration of the damaging impact of over-regulation. For excellence in both sectors, external control of the minutiae must be abandoned. The surest way, at least for now, of dismantling the centralised control crippling all education provision is to sever the inspectorate's collaborative relationship with the government. It is clear that OfSTED is very vulnerable to government influence and therefore susceptible to a situation in which safeguarding policy supersedes the safeguarding of learning. The next step is to develop an inspectorate with genuine independence—an inspectorate interested in education for education's sake rather than one welded to education for politics' sake.

Charterhouse Square School's OfSTED report is a landmark case (see Appendix 1). As this book seeks to demonstrate, OfSTED's failing of good schools encapsulates much of what is currently wrong with the state of education in this country. A single, though ever-changing and flawed, set of definitions of quality is creating failures out of successes in the private sector and successes out of failures in the state sector. While perhaps there is less concern about the fate of the privately educated, there is surely great consternation about the fate of Britain's most deprived pupils in the state sector. OfSTED's inspection regime is failing those children whose life chances hinge the most on good schooling. By forcing inappropriate and crippling government policy and performance targets on struggling schools, OfSTED is driving out dedicated teachers and the possibility of real progress (see Appendix 2).

As well as exposing the mechanisms and impact of government policy via OfSTED in the private sector, this research has sought to demonstrate why an agency which has been the subject of continual dissatisfaction on the part of educators not only survives but succeeds in further entrenching and expanding its powers. It seeks to explain why teachers in the state sector haven't revolted against the draconian and harmful dictation of their activities and why those in the private sector are not revolting now.

The research

Moving from the particular, a private school OfSTED report, to the general, New Labour's improvement drive, the aim of the research is to analyse how Charterhouse Square School's inspection report related to OfSTED's wider agenda, and how in turn this related to the government's national education strategy.

What therefore became the focus of the research was, firstly, an examination of the evidence demonstrating that private schools were being treated unfairly; secondly, a decipherment of the rationale behind it; and thirdly an exploration of the mechanisms which were enabling this rationale to be exercised.

Sources

The research is based on a combination of documentary evidence, primary data and academic literature. Documentary evidence has been gathered primarily from OfSTED and DfES literature, but also from the Independent Schools Inspectorate (ISI), the Independent Schools Council (ISC) and a number of teaching unions. Primary data comes from interviews with private and state school teachers and proprietors; teaching union representatives (from the National Association of Head Teachers, the Association of Teachers and Lecturers and the Professional Association of Teachers); Montessori and Steiner umbrella association representatives, representatives from associations in the Independent Schools Council (from the Society of Headmasters and Head Mistresses of Independent Schools, the Incorporated Association of Preparatory Schools and the Girls' Schools Association), OfSTED inspectors (an HMI, Assistant Inspector and former Lay Inspectors), ISI inspectors and local education authority (LEA) officials. The majority of these interviews were carried out by telephone. Additional interviews were carried out with former OfSTED Chief Inspector Chris Woodhead; the Chair of the Education and Skills Select Committee—the parliamentary body to which

OfSTED is accountable—Barry Sheerman MP; Master of Wellington College and biographer of Tony Blair, Anthony Seldon; head of the Centre for the Analysis of Risk and Regulation at the London School of Economics and leading analyst of audit, Professor Michael Power; director of the Curriculum, Evaluation and Management Centre at the University of Durham, Professor Peter Tymms; and head teacher of Summerhill School, Zoë Redhead. Academic literature, supplementary rather than central to the research, is taken from the fields of education, sociology, management & accounting and politics.

Strategy

The first leg of the research involved selecting a sample of independent primary school OfSTED reports with similar rulings to those of Charterhouse Square School. The idea was to cross-reference these reports in order to identify correlations between judged areas of weakness. Secondly, a sample of state primary school OfSTED reports was taken. In order to understand OfSTED's treatment of private schools, it was necessary to analyse OfSTED's focus and function in the state sector. The analytical backdrop to both sets of inspection reports was an examination of the OfSTED discourse as a whole. This very rapidly extended to an analysis of New Labour's education reform strategies since 1997.

The original intention was to limit the main body of the research to a documentary analysis of OfSTED's publications and reporting. However, scrutiny of the dynamics of the inspection process revealed increasing evidence of fundamental dysfunction in OfSTED's duties. It became clear that gaining a better understanding of the inspectorate's impact in the private sector would require informal accounts of inspection. The next stage of the research therefore required the collection of primary data from recently inspected independent schools. Supplementary to this, the inspection experiences of two more schools, one private and one state, were analysed as in-depth case studies.

The final leg of the research sought to anchor both state and private sectors' inspections in the context of New Labour government policy on education. Wishing to then build on my own empiricism, I sought a conceptual framework with which to illuminate the dynamics of the current education system. Max Weber's description of the functions of bureaucracy, combined with analysis stemming from Michel Foucault's examination of the power of regulatory discipline and surveillance, presented theoretical models pertinent to the deconstruction of OfSTED's organisation and mechanisms.

Every effort has been made to ensure that discussion on inspection materials is up-to-date. However, continual change in the particulars of OfSTED's strategy means that allowance must be made for subsequent alterations.

1
OfSTED the Enforcer

OfSTED's power, accrued via a combination of technique and authority, has enabled it to 'capture' the definition of quality in education, and therefore what is sought by both teachers and parents. Behind OfSTED's power lies a greater authority—the government. The inspectorate's lack of independence from the government has meant that it has become critical *to* the implementation of an improvement agenda, which as education watchdog it needs to be critical *of*. OfSTED's collaboration with the government's improvement drive has displaced objective and pluralistic criteria for determining quality in schools with centrally determined definitions. As a result, a monopoly has been created on what is acceptable in education: that which is accredited by OfSTED, and therefore that which is endorsed by the government. This organisation of the education system matters not simply because it entails a government stranglehold over school input and output, but because it has also often meant the nationwide enforcement of ill-advised and un-piloted education policy.

> ***The OfSTED handbooks for inspections indicate a clear model for evaluating effective teaching and learning. What is noticeable is that, with only the most minor of adjustments, this model of good teaching applies across the age phases.***
>
> *DfES, Teachernet, 'School Inspection', 2006*

The government's aim in taking control over school activity was to raise achievement, measured according to quantifiable targets: targets to demonstrate the effectiveness of the government's improvement strategy.[1] OfSTED's job, therefore, has become predominantly that of ensuring that a) this control is enforced, and that b) schools are reaching targets. This arrangement is, however, seriously malfunctioning in practice as well as principle as teachers have found that restrictive centrally-determined methods have not enabled them to meet the required targets. Teachers have thus found themselves compelled to create 'inspection trails' which falsely indicate their full implementation of government policy, in an attempt to reconcile compliance with doctrine with the attainment of performance targets. The worst-case scenario generated by these central pressures has been the coupling of falsified inspection evidence with teaching-to-the-test; in other words a discourse of fabrication (see Ball in chapter 5, 'Audit and Surveillance') in which the pupil and learning are virtually bypassed.

Yet despite its glaring defects, the organisation of the education system seems immovable. Teachers who refuse to participate in the initiative charade or the highly unpopular focus on targets are branded as standing in the way of their pupils' progress—when in fact these teachers' refusal to comply is in the interests of real learning. The main difficulty is that too much has been invested into the current organisation of the system, and too many people embroiled in its mechanisms, for it to be easily dismantled. Moreover, every attempt to salvage implementations politically and demonstrate the system's successes have entrenched it further. In 2004 researchers at the University of Leeds interviewed 115 Year 2 teachers who had had the opportunity to substitute formal assessment—Key Stage 1 SATs—with their own informal assessments. The researchers' conclusions demonstrate just how ingrained diktat has become, despite high levels of dissatisfaction:

> The high stakes of league tables and inspections have created a cowed profession when people for formal purposes follow everything to the letter, terrified of putting a foot wrong.[2]

External school inspection by national government *per se* is not a recent phenomenon, with the first inspections by Her Majesty's Inspectors of Schools (HMI) undertaken as early as 1839.[3] However OfSTED's establishment under John Major as an outcome of the 1992 Education Act signalled a new era of school inspection, both in scope and character. Inspection changed from being a process of advice-based support for individual schools to becoming a centralised system of utilitarian quality measurement and assessment.[4] The establishment of OfSTED signified the birth of a very different type of inspectorate. Chitty and Dunford describe HMI as a body perceived at the time to be: 'even-handed in its criticism, reporting as it found and criticising schools and the Government in equal measure'.[5] In the early 1990s, the Conservative government became concerned that HMI was: 'too close to the teachers and delivering too many messages that were uncomfortable to the Government'.[6] Consequently, under the direction of the serving Education Secretary, Kenneth Clarke, HMI was 'reformed', and OfSTED born. From that point onwards the remit of inspection was fundamentally altered: 'the inspectors' fire [was turned] almost entirely on to the teachers and away from the Government'.[7] Five years later, as a result of the 1996 Education Act, OfSTED's inspection remit was extended to include the private sector. The '96 Education Act made it a legal requirement for all private schools to be registered with the DfES. OfSTED's job was to 'inform' the DfES whether private schools fulfilled the regulations required for registration. Since then, the regulations OfSTED enforces have become more prescriptive and its remit widened. OfSTED now inspects 'the full range of services for children and young people, and life-long learning for all'.[8] As Barry Sheerman MP recently remarked, OfSTED's expansion has been comparable only to that of the British Empire.[9] Thus OfSTED, and therefore in effect the government, controls our education from cradle to grave.

> ***The profile of OfSTED is such that we are rarely out of the news.***
>
> *HMCI David Bell, OfSTED Annual Report 2004/2005*

OfSTED is a public service auditor: it is independent from its subjects, it gathers evidence and it passes judgement based on this evidence.[10] Yet OfSTED does far more than audit provision, it is a catalyst for conformity to the government's demands. A combination of monopoly over school accountability, tough methods and very public reporting provide the inspectorate with the power to produce this compliance. OfSTED's judgements are reported in the press, inspections have been known to lead teachers to nervous breakdown and reports to swing property-buying decisions for parents. Ferguson *et al.* have described OfSTED's inspection frameworks as having 'colonised' teachers' thinking by monopolising values in education.[11] Last year the then-Chief Inspector David Bell made a similar observation—although with a rather more positive spin to it:

> For schools, they [OfSTED's inspection frameworks] set out for the first time what inspectors saw as the key features of an effective school and how these features are recognised.[12]

The principle of OfSTED inspection works on the basis that high stakes—publicised outcomes and punitive repercussions for failure—equate with the pursuit of high standards. This propagates a public misconception that the stress and workload of inspection is an unavoidable bi-product of this noble quest. But as Coffey comments: 'the relationships between preparing for an inspection, the inspection process itself, and any fundamental and long-standing changes in classroom practice are rather tenuous.'[13] The adverse effects of a poor inspection report 'encourage teachers to work in ways during an inspection which would be neither viable nor possible to maintain.'[14] As well as presenting hugely elaborate and unrepresentative lessons, schools have been known to rent IT equipment and hide disruptive pupils.[15] Yet the consumers of OfSTED's reporting, parents, seem to be surprisingly unaware of the flaws in the inspection process. It is not understood that OfSTED does not simply seek evidence of good educational outcomes, but the application of specific teaching and learning practices. Increasing emphasis on the concept of 'parent power', for example, in newly proposed legislation giving parents 'new rights to trigger OfSTED inspections',[16] is exacerbating this blind faith in OfSTED's judgments and fostering an 'us' (OfSTED and parents) against 'them' (schools) relationship. The climax of this 'ganging-up' against teachers is OfSTED's 'pupil letters'. Inspectors now write to pupils summarising the inspection outcome—with lines such as: 'We have told your teachers they must try harder'.[17]

In 2005, Barbara Jones, the head teacher whose school topped the SATs league tables, told the press that the high test scores had been achieved by 'ignoring' government policy.[18] Much of the workload for inspection is in generating evidence for policies which have not been implemented because they are not effective for teaching and learning. Frequently, these policies are paperwork-based, such as very detailed lesson planning, tracking, target-setting and assessment recording.

OfSTED's highly punitive character has been central to compliance, real and artificial, with government policy. (In fact in many respects, a focus on the misguided principles of 'naming and shaming' schools in inspection has distracted us from being sufficiently critical about the basis of these judgements.) As the National Union of Teachers (NUT) has pointed out: 'teachers and schools prepare for evaluation out of fear, rather than commitment or enthusiasm'.[19] When policies are flawed and more likely to inspire resistance than commitment, fear becomes a fundamental tool.

Is OfSTED testing preparation for inspection or is it testing quality of education?

Head teacher of Melbury House preparatory school, in interview

OfSTED and the DfES

OfSTED may determine its inspection strategies to an extent (though even this freedom is constrained by budgetary restrictions) but the policies it enforces, and thereby the definitions of quality it adheres to, demonstrate that its autonomy from the government is very circumscribed. OfSTED would be better described as the *government's* education policy watchdog, rather than what it should be: the *stakeholders'* education policy and school standards watchdog. The inspectorate's current organisation means that ultimately it works not for the nation, but for the political party in power.

Since Tony Blair came to office in 1997, the government has seized power over the primary classroom. With the aim of rapidly improving schools, Blair decided that the most effective way to achieve this was by controlling schools through the dictation of teacher-activity. Government rhetoric alone would not guarantee that schools came on board the improvement drive, so OfSTED has become the enforcing agency of both government policies and government expectations. As David Bell once said: 'what is inspected tends to get done';[20] by inspecting compliance with DfES policy, OfSTED therefore secures the implementation of government pedagogy.

OfSTED's co-operation with the government's improvement agenda is in many respects very open, and where it is more opaque it is not deliberately deceptive. Very much part of the 'evangelical' battle for higher standards on one level, OfSTED is the proud missionary of the government's rapid improvement strategy. Hence the inspectorate's description of itself as a key partner 'at the heart of the government's strategy for high quality public services'.[21] Correspondingly, OfSTED's literature contains frequent references to the inspectorate as working 'on behalf' of the DfES,[22] indeed the OfSTED inspector interviewed for this research alternated repeatedly between 'we', OfSTED, and 'we', the DfES.[23] Yet, on the other hand, OfSTED's *independence* is asserted at length in much of its documentation: 'Our independence means you can rely on us for impartial information about the quality of education and care.'[24] Crucially, however, this independence is not from the government, and the meaning of 'information' is very specific.

One reason OfSTED appears to be a deceptively autonomous agency is because of its very genuine impartiality in relation to schools. OfSTED's treatment of schools is highly impartial, and on this basis its claim that it is 'not afraid to report as it finds'[25] is well founded. It is exactly the fact that OfSTED does report honestly however 'bad' a school is which is confusing: surely if the inspectorate were collaborating with the government it would sweep poor provision under the carpet? But it is not the inspectorate's scruples which are under fire here, it is the systemic relationship between OfSTED and the government—a relationship that is not exactly underhand, but rather vulnerable to manipulation. OfSTED's strict and inflexible detachment from schools has much to do with its equally inflexible *attachment* to the inspection framework which is based on government pedagogy. OfSTED's asserted impartiality is from *schools'*—not governmental—influence. Part of the problem lies in education policy legislation. Once a strategy becomes enshrined in law, it adopts both a coercive force and neutrality. OfSTED's enforcement of the government's policy is therefore perceived as the enforcement of statutory regulation—not party whim. This is illustrated by a comment by Woodhead: 'As Chief Inspector I was uneasy with the idea [of independent school inspection by OfSTED], but it was the law.'[26]

OfSTED would claim its autonomy from the government by pointing out that not only is its independence legislated for, but also that part of its remit is to 'advise on… the impact of particular innovations and government strategies'.[27] It would also point in its defence to a cross-party parliamentary committee which monitors its activities. First and foremost, OfSTED is a government department; the inspectorate has a gov.uk address and the chief inspector reports to the Secretary of State. Whatever the intention, this inherently jeopardises OfSTED's independence as it is institutionally part of the same political vehicle as the serving government. Secondly, OfSTED's evaluation of government education policy is unsatisfactory. True to its word of not having 'pulled our punches… on aspects of government policy where we do not think it is going quite as well as it might',[28] OfSTED is critical of the impact of misguided policy, but rarely criticises initiatives. OfSTED enforces the government's frequently un-piloted policies on schools too often unquestioningly. Rather than scrutinising reforms prior to their nationwide adoption, the inspectorate generally reserves criticism until *after* their implementation. At this stage, it is often too late to undo policies. This has arguably been the case with criticism of Foundation Stage profiling under Bell.[29] After a year of ensuring that schools performed the national assessments for five-year-olds, dubbed Foundation Stage 'profiling', OfSTED published a very critical report on them. Nevertheless, two years later, the government still requires schools to undertake the assessments, and therefore despite its expressed reservations, OfSTED is still ensuring their enforcement. OfSTED's criticism of outcomes policy also has a tendency to focus on their implementation: the fault resting with teachers rather than with the government's ideas. A pertinent example is when schools' poor teaching and leadership, rather than flaws in the Numeracy and Literacy Strategies and unrealistic targets, were blamed for the government's unlikelihood of meeting the 2006 SATs targets.[30]

On the few occasions where OfSTED has expressed concern at the proposal stage of a government policy, it has tended to be rather veiled. An illustration of this is the manner in which David Bell expressed his unease at plans to allow teaching assistants to take over class teaching. Bell clearly disagreed with the very concept, yet he pronounced his criticisms as his 'personal view'.[31]

Finally there is the impartiality ensured by the monitoring of OfSTED's activities by the Education and Skills Select Committee. The Committee's role is discussed in further detail below; however, in brief, its work focuses far more on monitoring the practical procedures and outcomes of OfSTED's activities than evaluating the fundamental principles of the inspection process. Nevertheless, asked about OfSTED's

> ***...although it could cite evidence of policy failure in inspection, OfSTED actually scrutinises policy very little.***
> *Chris Woodhead, in interview*

independence from the DfES, a member of the Committee, who wished to remain unnamed, pointed to former HMCI David Bell's recent appointment as Permanent Secretary of the DfES in answer: 'I think that says it all.'[32] According to Chris Woodhead: 'the independence of OfSTED depends on how much the chief inspector at the time protects this independence.'[33] Whilst it would be outrageous to accuse OfSTED's five chief inspectors to date of deliberate collusion with the government, their faithful participation with Blair's improvement drive essentially amounts to the same thing.

2
OfSTED in the State Sector

To illustrate OfSTED's role as enforcer of government policy, four state school inspection reports have been cross-referenced for commonalities and presented below. The reporting is from inspection carried out in 2004. Since 2004, state inspection and reporting arrangements have undergone significant change; however, this change might ultimately be described as merely cosmetic. Despite radical rhetoric, the principles of inspection and the foundation of the judgements remain little altered.

Each school's inspection team was made up of five inspectors, including one lay (non-professional) and one lead inspector. Inspections lasted three days and reports were on average 34 pages long.[1]

The strict parity in focus and structure of each report (extending to page numbers) is striking. Whilst it is to be expected that schools are judged on the same grounds, such uniformity can only leave little room for idiosyncrasies and individual context. This standardisation in format is one of many examples of OfSTED's rigidity in its approach to evaluating schools. Both in the former framework and the revised version, inspection teams are not encouraged to stray from official procedure by exercising any professional judgement.

OfSTED's reporting emphasises that inspection serves a wider purpose than simply judging a school. With each school having a good record of SATs performance, judgements go little further than attributing successes of the school to the successful implementation of government policy. Throughout the reports there is a heavy focus on school improvement since the last inspection. Implemented recommendations are particularly highly praised and their beneficial impact invariably asserted.[2] This aspect of the reporting highlights the self-legitimating nature of OfSTED's reporting; central to the inspection's function is assurance to the tax-payer that OfSTED is actively improving schools—hence their one-time motto 'Improvement through Inspection'. In a similar vein, the reporting attaches enormous importance to whether the school is providing 'value for money'.[3] Management teams that have succeeded in carrying money forward at the end of the school year are highly commended. The large sums saved lead one to wonder whether the repercussions of such economies are detrimental, or whether the expenditure in many primaries is unnecessary.[4]

'Plus ça change...'

Not only has OfSTED been working according to misguided principles, it has also been malfunctioning *within* its own framework. The artificial generation of required paperwork and the temporary introduction of recommended teaching techniques during the inspection period are commonplace responses to inspection. Furthermore, numerous pieces of research have found the stress of inspection to actually depress school performance.[5] Under David Bell's direction OfSTED underwent a series of changes which allegedly addressed the dysfunctional strains of the inspection process. In 2005, a new 'transformed' inspection framework for state schools was implemented. Crucially, little would change as the fundamental flaws of inspection—the underlying policies and control—were to remain.

OfSTED's revised inspection framework was born out of 'extensive consultation' with all 'stakeholders' in education.[6] The new framework was designed to reflect the government's 'new relationship with schools',[7] again highlighting the inspectorate's relationship with the government. Inspection's revised ethos would be reflected in new 'shorter, sharper' inspection arrangements with 'self-evaluation at the heart', and critically, OfSTED's 'lighter touch' approach

> ***We have tackled concerns head-on and introduced a radical new approach to inspection.***
>
> *David Bell, OfSTED Annual Report 2004/2005*

would 'reduce the burden of inspection on teachers'.[8]

OfSTED argued that these new arrangements would tackle all the issues responsible for OfSTED inspections' negative image. Short notice periods would mean that schools were no longer compelled to fabricate paperwork for the weeks prior to the inspection.[9] Less classroom observation would release the pressure to give teach-as-you've-never-taught-before performances. Management would be at the centre of scrutiny, easing demands on front-line teachers. Placing self-evaluation at the core of inspection would assuage the feeling of imposed external judgement: inspection would no longer be done 'to' a school but would become a 'collaborative' and constructive exercise.

The reality of the new arrangements has been rather different. Crucially, the premise of inspection has not changed, as the government's desire to control schools continues. Moreover, it is quite clear that the genuine motivation behind the alterations to inspection arrangements was a required expenditure cut of 20 per cent—approximately £40 million—by the academic year 2007-2008.[10]

As David Bell told the Education and Skills Select Committee: 'We believe you can have a lighter touch, smarter regulations and save money but actually continue to do a good job'.[11] And sure enough, OfSTED is continuing its regulatory duties not only more cheaply, but also more effectively. Arguably, the changes supposedly taking the sting out of the inspection regime have actually intensified rather than diluted OfSTED's role in ensuring centralised control over input and outcomes. Shorter inspection periods and shorter reports have upped the stakes. Instead of putting judgement into the hands of teachers, self-evaluation has become the most powerful regulatory tool in OfSTED's kit, with teachers now enforcing their own adherence to the

> ***... rarely has the spending of public money been under such careful scrutiny.***
>
> *HMCI David Bell, OfSTED Annual Report 2004/2005*

inspection framework. OfSTED's need to economise has meant securing a cheaper inspection workforce. This has been achieved largely through the regionalisation of inspection to five local 'regulatory inspection service providers' (RISPs).[12] A danger of this regionalised inspection is that a bid to address concerns about consistency between outsourced inspections will call for even greater rigidity. Thus, rather than weakening central control through devolution, regionalisation has very likely strengthened it.

Shorter inspections

> [I]t has concerned me to hear of high levels of stress and apprehension among staff. I am also concerned when I hear of the amount of preparation some schools have taken in advance of their OfSTED. We have tackled these concerns head on and introduced a radical new approach to inspection.
>
> HMCI David Bell,
> OfSTED Annual Report 2004/2005, Commentary

There is no longer time and money to gain a 'comprehensive' picture of schools, and therefore inspection now focuses on 'the key factors that drive school improvement'.[13] Less inspection time and contracted inspectors with less training mean that far greater emphasis has been placed on ticking off the required documented evidence: teaching and assessment records (plans and tracking evidence) and test and attainment results. Consequently OfSTED inspections now revolve around the head teacher presenting inspectors with a paper trail of the DfES policy with which their staff have been complying and the test results their pupils have been achieving—summarised in the self-

> ***There is no evidence that this [reducing inspection time] will help schools... [it] is likely to increase the 'high stakes' [nature of inspection]... and could lead to an increased emphasis on documentation requirements.***
> *National Union of Teachers: Response to the OfSTED consultation 'The Future of Inspection' 2004*

evaluation form. The new emphasis on management and leadership, with the principle that their quality 'is usually revealed by their impact',[14] means that test performance particularly, both in absolute and value added (progress) scores, has escalated in significance for inspection and for head teachers. (Once the proposed shorter inspection arrangements are in place, working on the principle of a 'more proportionate and risk based system of inspection',[15] this will be even more the case.)

The mitigation of direct strains on teachers, in the sense that teaching scrutiny is given less prominence, has not, however, taken the pressure off them. One teaching union official described how the new emphasis on leadership and management has led to 'onerous' regimes of constant lesson observations within schools, often accompanied by regimented weekly checks on documentary requirements such as planning and assessment files.[16] With more onus now placed on an individual—the head teacher—heads have become more vulnerable and therefore more 'effective' at getting their schools to produce the requirements. This greater pressure on head teachers is undoubtedly a contributing factor to the recent head teacher recruitment crisis.[17]

Self-evaluation

> ***In principle, self-evaluation gets full marks—but its implementation is something else.***
>
> *Alan Gotch, Association of Teachers and Lecturers, in interview*

The National Union of Teachers (NUT) declared themselves vindicated by the new inspection framework's emphasis on self-evaluation. In line with this, Chris Woodhead commented in interview that the introduction of self-evaluation was evidence of OfSTED and the government having 'caved in to the demands of the teaching unions', as 'inspection should be an *external* act.'[18] However, self-evaluation has not quite realised the vision of the unions, and indeed OfSTED's version of it is a dictated and therefore very much an 'external' process: schools can actually self-evaluate *wrongly*. A highly prescriptive self-evaluation form, extensive guidance on how to complete it and a published exemplar demonstrating how self-evaluation is done well, have taken away any school ownership of the exercise. Moreover, following the rules is imperative as 'poor' completion is interpreted by OfSTED as a sign of weak leadership.[19] In the private sector, schools are given what is termed a 'self-audit checklist' with which to ascertain their compliance to the DfES's regulations. 'Self-audit' would also be a more appropriate term for the state self-evaluation form. In its consultation response, the National Union of Teachers (NUT) warned OfSTED that 'prescribed' self-evaluation forms should be avoided as they ran the risk of 'distorting a school's own work': precisely what has happened.[20] The union was also concerned that self-evaluation would create extraneous work unless it was accommodated within schools' existing documentation.[21] Once again, the self-evaluation forms are indeed very lengthy with reports of their taking as long as 40 hours to complete.[22]

As Chris Keates, General Secretary of the National Association of Schoolmasters Union of Women Teachers (NASUWT), has remarked, OfSTED's form of self-evaluation would better be interpreted as 'trying to get teachers to do the regulatory work themselves'.[23] Far from being a process of reflection, it is a process of self-regulation. Since its introduction, the NUT has complained that heads feel penalised for filling in their self-evaluation honestly. In OfSTED's piloting of the self-evaluation forms, schools were regarded as portraying themselves in an 'overly positive' light.[24] Head teachers were not measuring their schools rigidly enough against OfSTED's requirements.

Shorter inspection notice

Under the old framework schools were given six to eight weeks notice of an OfSTED inspection. These weeks were

> *We are giving virtually no notice of inspection, so there should be no unnecessary preparation for an inspection; we will serve children much better if we see childcare settings and schools as they really are.*
>
> HMCI David Bell, OfSTED Annual Report 2004/2005

essentially to give schools time to prepare for inspection. The problem was that much of this preparation was made purely for the purposes of the inspection. This was particularly the case for documented procedure, for example planning and assessment documents, and the appearance of the school. Teachers would produce one-off elaborate planning and assessment, and create very time-consuming displays. Once the inspectors had departed, these activities would often cease.

By removing the notice period, OfSTED declared that inspection 'performance' would be avoided: schools would no longer have time to fabricate an inspection trail. But seeing the notice period as the root of fabrication for inspection is to miss the problem—the stipulation of unachievable and/or useless directives. Consequently no-notice inspection has not eliminated fabrication as the directives continue. The charade is by no means dead—it has simply become integral to daily activity. Indeed, concern has been expressed that a three-year inspection cycle may well lead to far worse, *year-long* pre-inspection tension and paper trail creation, now twice as frequently.[25]

Shortened reports

The length of reports has been reduced to around 11 pages. Tightening the focus of inspections and shortening the report has had the effect of paring judgements down to summarised descriptions with a greater emphasis on what are considered the essentials: outcomes, improvements made since the last inspection and the school's capacity to improve further. Both outcomes and improvement are married to the concept of the school's 'value for money'. When outcomes themselves are not the direct focus, the attention is on how strategies have produced them. Teaching, for example, is not judged as an activity in itself but under the heading 'Achievement and Standards', where, again, quantifiable performance is the basis of judgement.

The new reports reassert the idea of inspection as being about a school's fit to the standard template and its fit in comparison to other schools—but not about the individual school itself. As well as a grade between one and four now punctuating every section of the report, the graded overview of the whole school is now made up of new categories. This is a summary of the full range of factors that, in OfSTED's view, determine the quality of education. De-contextualised judgements with a small grade range make the chart insightful only in terms of broad comparison—increasingly the purpose of inspection. Moreover, some of the judgements in the chart, for example: 'How well learners develop workplace and other skills that will contribute to their future economic well-being'[26] are meaningless, if not absurd, in primary school reporting. (Although this example is clearly a politically loaded addition, a reminder of the economic gains to be had from investment in education.)

The new arrangements keep teachers skilfully under control, whilst ostensibly giving them greater autonomy—and slicing off the necessary chunk of expenditure to boot. Highly standardised inspection with minimised manpower and professional judgement can only tick off requirements from a list and note down standardised performance. This is exactly the government's desired goal, and thus OfSTED's new framework is even more effective for its purposes.

Overall, MacDonald's description of the inspectorate is even more pertinent than when it was published in 2000:

> [An] ad hoc inspectorate chosen from an approved list and paid daily rates to carry out periodic evaluations of individual school compliance and performance. Thus failing schools (are) identified, publicly shamed and threatened with closure, much like a bankrupt business.[27]

With the private sector now also implicated in the government's 'improvement drive', the concept of the bankrupt business is more reality than simile; OfSTED's power over public opinion means a choice between compliance with government stipulations, however at odds they are with a school's own policies, or the loss of custom and the threat of closure.

3
OfSTED in the Private Sector

> ***Schools don't cause OfSTED concern for very long: either they change or close—and if parents see a bad report, schools won't last.***
>
> *OfSTED inspector of independent schools, in interview*

Of the approximately 2,500 independent schools in England, roughly 1,200 are inspected directly by OfSTED, with the other 1,300, those in associations belonging to the Independent Schools Council (ISC), inspected by the OfSTED-monitored Independent Schools Inspectorate (ISI).[1] ISC member schools are required to comply with the DfES's statutory Independent School Standards, just as non-association schools must. Of the 1,200 (approximately) schools inspected directly by OfSTED, around 800 are mainstream providers, roughly 600 of which are schools catering for primary level (4-11 year-olds).[2]

Although DfES regulation for independent schools was first introduced via the 1944 Education Act, it was not until legislative changes brought in by the 2002 Education Act, effective from September 2003, that the private sector felt the force of government regulation on everyday practice.

> ***The 2002 Education Act was extremely powerful: previously it was possible for anyone to set up a school. You couldn't stop them from starting up and closing them down was very difficult.***
>
> *OfSTED inspector, in interview*

With the 2002 Education Act came a prescribed set of written standards set by the DfES and, all importantly, the publication of private school inspection reports.[3] Whereas previously it had been 'down to... parents to decide whether provision was suitable for their children', the regulation and reporting now did so for them.[4] In addition, schools now had to apply to be registered before they could open. Whereas in the past schools had been able to start up and function simply by applying for provisional registration, now schools would face a preopening visit followed by an inspection within their first year.[5] Thereafter, schools would be subject to routine inspections every six years. Those that 'did badly' would be 'followed up more frequently' to ensure that they implemented the required changes.[6]

> ***OfSTED has had an enormous impact on independent schools… and the DfES is delighted: they really feel they are being moved on.***
>
> *OfSTED inspector, in interview*

Nowhere is OfSTED's collaborative role with the government more apparent than in private school inspections. In the private sector OfSTED's *raison d' être* is to enforce government policy. Whilst OfSTED implements the regulations, the regulatory *authority* is clearly defined in documents as being the DfES,[7] prompting an interviewed OfSTED inspector to comment that it was not OfSTED but 'the DfES which is the regulator of schools'.[8] Thus OfSTED is the doer and the DfES the thinker (in a relationship not dissimilar to that of Trotsky and Lenin). OfSTED's 'implementer' role explains why the interviewed OfSTED inspector was enthusiastic about legislative moves which made the regulations more legally binding: upping the force of regulation facilitates OfSTED's job. Indeed the inspector described the more 'powerful' legislation as 'excellent for us [OfSTED]'.[9]

> ***Independent schools must meet the requirements of detailed regulations in order to retain their registration. These schools' ability to meet the regulations must be reported in detail to the regulatory authority [DfES].***
>
> *DfES: 'Inspection of Non-association Independent Schools'*

Despite the fact that SATs results in the private sector are generally 20 per cent higher than the national average and that over 50 per cent of independent school GCSE entries score A or A* compared to around 13 per cent from the state sector,[10] the government still considers it justifiable to dictate regulatory requirements concerning the education private schools provide. Indeed, there is an inherent reluctance to recognise the successes of private sector pupils as the successes of private school provision. This is demonstrated in an OfSTED overview of independent schools published the year after New Labour came into power. One section of the report discusses pupils' attentiveness and good behaviour in class defined by OfSTED as 'pupils' positive attitudes'. Rather than attributing these positive attitudes to effective teaching, the opposite position is taken: '(Positive pupil attitude) makes the task of teaching relatively straightforward; indeed these positive attitudes occasionally compensate for teaching which would otherwise be ineffective.'[11] In 1998, OfSTED inspected 411 independent schools; 60 schools were reported as causing 'considerable concern'.[12] The chief cause for this 'concern' was failure to meet the requirements regarding instruction.[13] This, significantly, was before the 2002 Education Act whereby 'requirements for instruction' would become considerably more prescriptive.

The DfES has drawn up seven sections of Independent School Standards, and it is OfSTED's job to enforce compliance with these standards.[14] The standards are set out in seven categories, which can be broken down into a total of 96 regulations. The regulatory sections are as follows:

- the quality of education provided by the school, which is broken down into two sub-categories, the quality of the curriculum and the quality of the teaching and assessment;
- the spiritual, moral, social and cultural development of pupils;
- the welfare, health and safety of the pupils;
- the suitability of the proprietor and staff;
- the suitability of the premises and accommodation;
- the quality of information for parents and other partners;
- the effectiveness of the school's procedures for handling complaints.

Notably this is the order that the regulatory categories are reported on: with the quality of education, rather than health and safety issues, first.

Not only are the regulations extensive, the details within them do not equate with a broad notion of minimum standards. Generally, the regulations are in themselves specific, for example, regulation 1:3:g, a requirement under the heading 'the quality of education provided by the school':

> Demonstrate that a framework is in place to assess pupils' work regularly and thoroughly and use the information from that assessment to plan teaching so that pupils can progress.[15]

In instances where there appears to be greater scope for interpretation, potential for varied interpretation is displaced by current DfES dogma. For example, also in 'the quality of education provided by the school, regulation 1:3:c states: 'The teaching at the school shall involve well-planned lessons, effective teaching methods, suitable activities and wise management of class time.' As will be shown below, OfSTED's translation of 'well-planned', 'effective teaching methods' and 'suitable activities' is highly inflexible.[16] Moreover, on top of the official regulations are OfSTED's 'recommendations'. In their reports, OfSTED frequently makes suggestions which 'whilst not required by the regulations, the school might wish to consider... for development'. In light of the power relationship between the inspectorate and schools, these recommendations are most likely implemented.[17]

The level of stipulated detail means that schools can fail regulatory requirements and consequently receive an unfavourable inspection report purely on the basis of not doing things 'the government's way'. According to OfSTED, the only reason that the private sector has retained the freedom not to implement the National Curriculum, and thereby not be forced to emulate state arrangements even further, is due to the 'powerful faith schools lobby which objected to subjects like music.'[18]

> ***Upped regulation and requirement to publish reports has had a major impact on provision—making the job of inspection much more powerful.***
> *OfSTED inspector, in interview*

David Bell, former Chief Inspector, under whose direction the publication of private school reports was first introduced, was very aware that the publication of OfSTED's independent school reporting would have a major impact on private provision. Addressing an audience of independent school head teachers in 2003, he declared that private schools would 'have to do better', as 'while the independent sector contains very many schools that are very good, it also includes a number of schools that are among the worst in the country.'[19] A driving force for this improvement would be the publication of schools' OfSTED reports.[20] Bell's proposal that schools do 'better' was heavily loaded. What constituted this improvement was very specific: greater adherence to the DfES's current pedagogy brought in by more prescriptive regulation. The following year, after the enforcement of this level of prescription was underway, Bell subsequently commented that: 'The need to meet the requirements of the regulations, reinforced by inspections, has improved the quality of [private] provision.'[21] While no claims can be made that private schools are uniformly good, the independent sector does have the rigour of the market on its side: poor provision is unlikely to retain custom. The private sector also has higher performance on its side. However in a direct admission that government regulation of the private sector was to become heavy-handed, Bell disagreed that market forces regulated private provision sufficiently:

> One of the arguments for lighter regulation in the independent sector is that market forces will result in poor schools going out of business and good schools prospering. However, to work effectively a market needs reliable and easily available information. And for consumers to exercise choice in a market, they require good information.[22]

The problem with Bell's equation is the nature of the information: where improvement is necessary it should not automatically be regarded as solely achievable by emulating state-sector methodologies. Moreover, where provision does *not* emulate state methods it should not be regarded as in need of improvement.

It is of little surprise, in light of the level of government dictation about what is acceptable, that alternatives to state pedagogy have become limited in number and in scope, in both the state and the private sector. In 2003 Dr Robert Bell, a former researcher in education at the Open University and current vice-president of the European Forum for Freedom in Education (EFFE),[23] carried out an evaluation of the UK's schools system. Bell identified five 'deficits' in the English system, each of which related to the limited opportunities for pedagogy that strayed from the government's paths. His observed weaknesses were as follows:

- the National Curriculum narrowed the freedom of schools;
- pedagogical minorities such as Waldorf schools repeatedly failed to gain admittance into the state system;
- there were very few 'alternative' schools;
- there were no subsidies for independent schools;
- and crucially, independent schools were restricted by state control.[24]

Summerhill triumphant?

Summerhill, A.S. Neill's famous 'progressive' private school in Suffolk, is one of the few remaining alternative education providers in the country. It is also the only independent school to have successfully taken legal action against the government in protest at the DfES's regulations for the private sector. Bearing in mind the rigid nature of the DfES's regulations for independent schools, it is of little surprise that a school whose underlying principle is voluntary class attendance failed to fulfil statutory requirements. Refusing to alter its provision, Summerhill repeatedly failed to comply with the regulations in inspection after re-inspection until the school finally took their case to the Independent Schools Tribunal in 2000. Summerhill put forth the case that compliance to the government's Independent School Standards disabled the school's own goals. With the help of considerable media publicity and public support—and £120,000 in legal fees—Summerhill won the case to continue running the school without fully complying with the regulations. However, revealingly, the secretary of state at the time, David Blunkett, released a public statement announcing that the DfES had 'come to an agreement' with Summerhill, and that they were 'very pleased' with the changes Summerhill had agreed to make. Zöe Redhead, A.S. Neill's daughter and head teacher of Summerhill, argues that the DfES's statement deliberately covered up the defeat of the government's authority. Summerhill had in fact only agreed to make several health-and-safety-related changes, and apart from that has continued to run the school fulfilling only two out of the DfES's seven regulations, 'the quality of education provided by the school' not being one of them.[25] Yet while Summerhill was triumphant, the case had repercussions for the independent sector's autonomy. Summerhill's victory was undoubtedly a catalyst for the government to up regulation in the private sector in 2002.

> ***My Lords, since when has it been the policy of the government to take a view about the philosophy and education of private schools? This is a school which attained 75 per cent A to C passes in 1998 and 63.9 per cent in 1999. Those figures are well above the national averages. There is no truancy; and there is the highest possible level of parental satisfaction with the school. When those parents are paying their money and know what they are paying for, who are we to take a different view about the philosophy of education in a private school.***
>
> *Baroness Blatch, House of Lords, June 1999*

Whilst Summerhill's case is somewhat extreme due to the unconventional nature of its provision, it nevertheless illustrates the difficulty of resisting the force of the government's regulations—even with considerable support and resources to hand. Clearly, legal action requiring this level of expense and publicity is not an option available for the majority of OfSTED-inspected private schools. Furthermore, because contestations are generally likely to revolve around the dictation of pedagogical detail rather than a wholly different educational philosophy, most schools would find it much harder to fight the system as the basis for their complaints would be less neatly definable. In this respect there is more hope for schools which have a distinctly different and documented ethos, for example Steiner and Montessori schools. Indeed the Montessori Schools Association recently succeeded in getting what they considered to be an unfair OfSTED report removed from OfSTED's website, which, as a member of their organisation remarked, is 'unheard of'.[26] However, this was after considerable expense in hiring a consultant and with the support of a lobby group. For the small independent school that is genuinely independent from other schools and organisations, resistance is futile. Thus, as the head teacher of one such school, South School, commented: 'It's just not worth battling against [compliance to regulation] if you can afford to make the changes—otherwise they'll [OfSTED] just come back.'[27] With the expense of inspection already very difficult to accommodate for many small schools, protest which might lead to additional expense is to be avoided.[28]

Overall it is the smaller, less well-off schools that find it more difficult to take the DfES's regulations in their stride. These types of school bear the brunt of the system, having to fork out sizeable chunks of their budget to pay for an inspection in which they are told to spend more money on implementations they very often consider unnecessary or even detrimental.

The government's relationship with OfSTED is severely infringing on the private sector's liberties by forcing nominally autonomous provision to conform to a particular pattern: that of current state educational doctrine. Whilst OfSTED states that 'inspectors do not expect schools to conform to a common pattern of provision', this is greatly undermined by the initial proviso: '*subject to a school's compliance with statutory requirements*'.[29] OfSTED's inspection of private schools claims to fully observe the independent sector's right to remain autonomous. However, the statutory requirement of compliance to the DfES's fastidious regulations means that independent schools are finding their practices constrained by the state template of 'good' teaching.

This interplay between a single acceptable definition of quality, OfSTED's influence in the public domain and the private school's dependence on its market status, means that the independent sector can do little but silently comply. Private schools thus find themselves in the perverse situation in which they are compelled to comply with DfES regulation in order to retain their reputations as good schools, and thereby their market popularity—popularity and success which was *not* gained by fulfilling DfES criteria. What is more, they are now finding themselves compelled to implement many of the distractions from frontline activity which have been so detrimental in the state sector.

> Government intervention is only legitimate where government money has been invested… [however] there is definitely fear on the part of independent schools to be critical of government regulation as it makes them appear not to be accountable.[30]

Fuelling this perception (which was heightened by the fact that the interviewee asked to be made anonymous), was the interviewed OfSTED inspector's observation that: '…the good schools co-operate and only the bad ones don't.'[31] Thus, together with the market repercussions of an unfavourable inspection report, this has been sufficient impetus for private schools to bow to government intervention.

The samples

The OfSTED inspection experiences of independent schools were analysed through a combination of official and unofficial data. The main sources of evidence were a sample of private school inspection reports and a sample of interviews with representatives of private schools which had recently undergone inspection. Weaving the latter informal accounts of inspection into an analysis of the published reports allowed a three-dimensional picture of the inspection process to emerge.

The samples consisted of a total of eight primary-level independent schools. Four inspection reports were scrutinised and four additional schools were interviewed, as well as their reports being examined. The gathered evidence spans two years, with inspections in the report sample carried out in the academic year 2003/2004, and inspections in the interview sample carried out in the academic year 2005/2006. Unlike in the state sector, OfSTED's arrangements for private school inspection have remained almost entirely unchanged. Nonetheless, OfSTED is proposing to alter private school inspections in line with changes made in the state sector. However, while cost-cutting has been a key catalyst for the new state arrangements, the fact that independent schools pay for inspection themselves means there is not the same pressure.

The four inspection reports were published in 2004, with schools selected, not at random but on the basis of not having fulfilled all the DfES's regulatory requirements. Each report was a write-up of a routine inspection, to decide whether the school should be allowed continued registration with the DfES. The aim of the analysis was to identify any emergent patterns regarding the weaknesses which had caused the schools to fail regulations. The resulting sample consisted of four schools from across the country: Gower House in London; Lyonsdown in Hertfordshire; Beehive Preparatory in Essex; and The Dower House School in Shropshire. Additional background information on these schools such as their academic performance, which was not included in their OfSTED reports, was also gathered.

The interviewed schools, on the other hand, were selected entirely at random from reports published on OfSTED's website at the end of 2005. The resultant sample produced a mixed set of judgements, with one school fulfilling all but one regulation, another fulfilling five out of the seven regulations and the remaining two failing over half. Only one school out of the four fulfilled the regulation regarding 'the quality of education provided by the school'. Three of the schools had undergone routine inspections and one school a re-inspection to monitor the implementation of its last 'action plan'. This school had failed to fulfil the necessary regulations six times over three years; the outcome of its last inspection was that it was required to address 22 areas of regulation.[32] The names of the schools have been changed to West, North, South and East Schools.

West School was a mixed non-selective school in Bristol with 123 full-time pupils and annual fees of approximately £4,000;[33] West School fulfilled all but one requirement, 'the welfare, health and safety of the pupils'. North School in London was also a non-selective mixed school and had 38 full-time pupils and annual fees of approximately £8,500; North School failed to meet four out of seven of the requirements, 'the quality of education provided', 'the spiritual, moral and cultural development of pupils', 'the welfare, health and safety of pupils' and 'the suitability of the proprietor and staff'. South School was a non-selective mixed school in Gloucestershire with 58 pupils on roll and annual fees of around £5,000; South School failed all the regulations except for 'the welfare, health and safety of pupils'. East School in Bedfordshire was a non-selective, mixed faith-based school with 45 pupils and annual fees of under £1,500; East School failed to fulfil two out of seven of the requirements, 'the quality of education provided' and 'the suitability of the premises and accommodation'.

The interviews sought to address three broad questions.

Firstly, what were the schools' views on private school inspection by OfSTED? Secondly, how did their experiences of the inspection process relate to their school's published inspection reports? And lastly, how had OfSTED inspection affected the daily running of the school in preparation for, during and since inspection? The issues which arose out of the samples were remarkably similar, particularly in the sense that the areas of implementation which the interviewed private schools especially objected to were the areas which OfSTED found to be the weakest in its reporting.

The final piece of the jigsaw was to incorporate OfSTED's perspective into an account of the independent school inspection process. This was done by analysing OfSTED's literature on independent inspection and by interviewing an HMI. HMIs are now OfSTED's only full-time and centrally employed inspectors. The remarks have been anonymised as, on reflection, the inspector did not wish them to be attributed to her.

The nature of OfSTED's public reputation and influence is such that the schools where a representative has been interviewed have had to be disguised with pseudonyms and their reports un-referenced. Strict confidentiality had to be guaranteed for these interviewees to openly discuss their inspections. One fear of identification was that criticism of the inspection process might lead to adverse repercussions for the school; the other main concern was that OfSTED might disapprove of the ways a school had prepared for inspection, also potentially leading to adverse consequences.

The widespread fear generated by the OfSTED discourse is a powerful illustration of the command the inspectorate has over education—now including the private sector. The result is not only that schools, state and private, feel compelled to comply with regulations they disagree with, but the influence of the inspectorate means that schools feel unable even to be openly critical of them. Despite the widespread dissatisfaction with OfSTED's private school inspections expressed in the interviews, according to OfSTED there are just 'one or two' formal complaints a year.[34] This fact is of little surprise in light of the HMI's assertions that: 'If the inspector has followed the framework there is no grounds [*sic*] for complaint'. Moreover, the HMI also dismissively remarked that the few complaints made tended to be '...along the lines of "we are better than you say"', and consequently were generally not upheld.[35]

Findings

> ***OfSTED comes in [to private schools] with a very limited remit.***
>
> *South School*

Private school reports are several pages shorter than state school reports. This sounds like a reasonable disparity considering that fewer directives must be applicable to private schools in view of their greater autonomy. However, not only have the DfES's regulations for the independent sector become virtually as extensive as those of the state sector (the interviewed OfSTED inspector described the private sector as 'at least as rigorously monitored by OfSTED as maintained [state] schools'),[36] more importantly, private schools are potentially being judged on *more*. By being both government monitored and market-led, independent schools must fulfil not only the DfES's regulations but also their own goals to ensure their popularity.

Throughout OfSTED's literature on independent school inspection there are references to private sector inspection and reporting as also examining the extent to which a school achieves its own goals.[37] However, in its more perfunctory literature, OfSTED describes the aims of independent school inspection as being:

> [T]o ensure that the school is complying with the requirements of the regulations for registration under section 163 [of the Education Act 2002] and, where it does not, to tell the school what it must do to improve.[38]

Brief reports—and inspections—in which the DfES's regulations are heavily prioritised render the scope of the judgements too narrow to accommodate properly the school's own definitions of success—or even the market's. The Independent Schools Inspectorate (ISI) reports, in comparison, discussed below, accommodate more satisfactorily both the DfES's regulatory requirements and the schools' own aims. Although reports have been considerably shortened in the revised ISI inspection regime which came into force in January 2006, their inspections and reporting continue to go 'above and beyond' OfSTED's, and this is a main reason why their system is preferable for independent schools.[39] The narrow scope of inspection matters particularly for the OfSTED-inspected private school because, once the inspection report is published, the school is publicly defined according to this very narrow ruling. The interviewed inspector neatly encapsulated this issue by declaring that: 'The extent to which the DfES's regulations are met shows how good a school is'.[40] This is clearly very unfair for schools whose provision does not match the DfES's expectations, but does fulfil its own—and above all those of its 'customers', the parents. Before the 2002 regulations for independent schools came into force OfSTED undertook a consultancy survey with stakeholders in the independent schools sector. The point of the consultation was to gather feedback on the new requirements of private schools. One question in the consultation asked: 'do you agree that the evaluation schedule will capture the essence of what the school is about'. Fewer than half the respondents agreed. OfSTED's response to this was that: 'schools are reminded that inspectors are judging them against a set of common regulations which apply to all independent schools, irrespective of type and ethos, and have been introduced to secure the health, welfare and educational progress of all pupils in the independent sector'.[41]

Judged weaknesses

Overall, the specific area of greatest contention, and indeed the area most criticised by OfSTED, was meeting the requirements regarding 'the quality of the education provided'. This regulation is split into two sub-headings, one concerning curriculum content, and the other methods of teaching and assessment. Three out of the four interviewed schools failed this regulation, as did all the schools in the report sample.[42]

Each school in the report sample was criticised on the basis of their curriculum and teaching strategies. Within the section 'the quality of the curriculum', weaknesses ranged from insufficient ICT (information and communications technologies) provision,[43] inadequate planning techniques[44] and limited and inappropriate resources,[45] to an overly narrow curriculum[46]. Many of these weaknesses were also replicated in the interview sample. The extensive range of criticisms in just one sub-category out of seven areas of regulation demonstrates how far-reaching the stipulations have become. This level of central dictation is very much at odds with OfSTED's private sector remit which in principle does not interfere with schools' right to remain 'free to decide for themselves how they operate and how they conduct their daily affairs...'[47]

In the second part of the regulations relating directly to the education provided, in the section headed 'the quality of teaching and assessment', each school, across report and interview samples, was reprimanded in some way for straying from DfES methodologies, from lesson delivery to marking style. More specifically, the schools failed to comply with this area of regulation on grounds of insufficient assessment and differentiation,[48] inadequate and/or inappropriate marking,[49] over-directed teaching,[50] unsatisfactory planning,[51] and over-emphasis on secondary school entrance preparation.[52]

The backdrop to these judgements must be continually emphasised: all eight schools in the sample were popular and successful schools. In spite of, or very often *because* of, their shortcomings in relation to OfSTED's template, each school fulfilled their own goals and held a good academic record.[53] What is striking is that OfSTED acknowledges this success with remarks such as: 'the pupils' overall achievement is good and the quality of teaching is good'. Yet in the very same report planning and assessment techniques are judged to be inadequate.[54] The importance of compliance with set procedure, in other words, has not only superseded the importance of outcome, it has blinded logic. Clearly if planning and assessment were poor, so would be teaching and achievement.[55] This example seems to encapsulate all that is wrong with OfSTED's inspections of the private sector.

> ***All teachers mark pupils' work conscientiously, although much of this takes the form of ticks, marks and brief comments.***
>
> *Gower House School OfSTED inspection report, 'The quality of education provided by the school: the quality of teaching and assessment'*

The fundamental problem with the DfES's regulations for private schools and the manner in which they are implemented by OfSTED is that they coerce schools into emulating the practices of the state sector. Criticisms about schools' methods of marking are a useful illustration. The alleged weakness on this issue was not that schools were neglecting to mark work *per se*, but that the technique employed was not the one currently advocated by the DfES. Yet looking back at an OfSTED overview of the quality of independent school provision from 1998: 'the rigorous correction of errors' was at the time seen to 'contribute significantly to pupils' progress'.[56] In other words, a method of straightforward correction once recognised as effective is now discredited because the DfES has adopted an alternative approach. The point is less about the pedagogy and more about the principle. This example illustrates the arbitrary—as well as illegitimate—nature of the government's intervention. In the same vein, commenting on assessment, the interviewed inspector remarked that: 'Independent schools don't tend to be strong on assessment: they *do* plenty of assessment, but they don't do it *right*.'[57] The effectiveness of 'wrong' ways is irrelevant.

Paperwork

OfSTED's vision of 'proper'[58] assessment, as is so often the case with DfES dogma, is writing it down in great detail. Whilst schools in the samples were often commended for the intimate knowledge of their pupils' learning, ultimately the only acceptable evidence of pupil knowledge was that which was *documented*.[59] Whilst the need to monitor children's learning is indisputable, the DfES places far too much emphasis on formal and standardised mechanisms for doing so. Moreover, justification for formal assessment procedures in state schools is weaker in the private sector. In a context with a high staff—as well as often pupil—turnover (as in state schools)[60] teachers have less opportunity to develop detailed knowledge of their pupils. As a result there is a better case for documenting information about pupils in order that it be made available to successive teachers.

In the private sector, on the other hand, the teaching force is considerably more stable. Thus, if assessment requirements are interpreted as strategies to mitigate the issue of discontinuity in the state sector, they are being inappropriately imposed on private schools. However, the value of constant documented assessment even in the state sector is questionable. As well as alienating state-school teachers, superfluous formal assessment and tracking is squeezing out vital *in*formal methods. The mere fact that the regulatory sub-heading in the independent school regulations is 'the quality of teaching *and assessment*' highlights both the importance attached to assessment as well as how it has become artificially separated from teaching. Assessment is now designed to be behind-the-scenes, divorced from frontline activity.

In 2002 Professors Maurice Gaton and John MacBeath undertook a study examining the ways in which primary school teaching had changed over the last three decades.[61] Although school days have become longer, and teachers spend more time working 'after hours', the researchers found that time pressures now made it impossible for teachers to go through work with pupils and give one-to-one feedback.[62] The researchers clearly regarded this decline of valuable informal assessment strategies as a penalty of prescription and curriculum over-load. Yet, where these informal practices have survived in the private sector, far from being credited as beneficial, they are being undermined.

> ***A significant improvement in the development of assessment is the introduction of promising procedures to track pupils' progress throughout Key Stages 1 and 2. Staff have received recent training and the new system starts in January 2006.***
>
> *East School inspection report, 'The quality of education provided by the school: the quality of the teaching and assessment'*

Overall it was schools' lack of 'documentation' in both the report and interview sample that was their biggest downfall. Even where the required activities were being undertaken, as shown for example by outcome, the paperwork to prove it was required. Precedence to procedure over outcome meant that informal or alternative methods were discredited or simply disallowed. The first order goal, of good educational outcomes, was perversely superseded by the second order goal of how these goals must be achieved.

Much compliance with the DfES's regulations involves documenting activity, be it in the form of schemes of work, planning, assessment or recorded evidence relating to other areas of school life in policy documents and risk assessments. Subsequently, inspection focuses heavily on whether schools have generated the prerequisite paper trail. Although getting schools to document activity is designed to ensure that they are actually carrying the activities out, just as in the state sector this was often not the case, with evidence created solely for the purpose—and duration—of the inspection.

West School felt that the emphasis on 'documented evidence' was 'very top-heavy, with much more interest in paperwork and comparatively little in watching lessons'.[63] However, unlike in the state sector, documented evidence is predominantly used to demonstrate procedure rather than performance. Whereas performance indicators, such as SATs results at primary level, are central to OfSTED's reporting in state schools, the relative insignificance of quantifiable achievement in private reporting is striking. While, for example, four of the schools from the two samples took SATs with outcomes consistently above the national average, test attainment was only discussed in one of the reports.

> ***Bureaucracy does commonly come to the fore of complaints [from private schools]: but if it's the law it must be done.***
> *OfSTED inspector, in interview*

From the interview sample it was clear that schools were most resistant to the bureaucracy required by the regulations because it was seen as contributing the least constructively to teaching and learning. With paperwork overload a significant contributor to the staff retention crisis in the state sector,[64] it is ironic that private schools are being penalised for not doing *enough*.

The requirements to produce reams of paperwork, the benefits of which are often unclear, such as 100 'risk assessments'—including an assessment of the potential hazards of blowing a whistle[65]—is a very intrusive distraction from the frontline. It is a worrying indictment of government education policy that those schools with more time to focus on their pupils are presented as inadequate.

The dictation of what is taught and how it is taught

Other weaknesses identified in the report sample were mirrored by 'inadequacies' the interviewed schools found themselves having to address—either in response to informal pre-inspection advice or in response to formal inspection judgements. Each of the interviewed schools was in some respect coerced via inspection into altering its teaching-related arrangements, from what they taught to how they taught. This was done either in preparation for inspection and/or in carrying out requirements in the action plan, post-inspection.

> ***If there is a box for it, it must be ticked, and if something doesn't have a box it's ignored.***
> *North School*

It was, however, clear from the interviews that, as educators, the inspectors could see the benefits of alternative arrangements which did not comply with regulation. Yet their role as implementers of regulatory requirements meant that their duty was to enforce these rather than evaluate provision objectively or professionally. In this respect inspectors were merely technicians in the inspection process. In South School, for example, ICT provision was formally reported as a weakness—a recurring failing across the schools in the samples.[66] Yet during the inspection the lead inspector had told South School that 'personally' she thought their ICT arrangements were good. The regulations however, meant that her 'hands were tied' with regard to reporting.[67]

> ***When I challenged a judgement in discussion, the inspectors shrugged their shoulders saying they simply had 'to follow the rules and tick the boxes'.***
> *West School*

Together with frequent examples of 'off the record' advice and accounts of the inspectors as 'friendly and helpful', it was evident that the rigid and draconian element of the inspection process lay not so much in the inspection teams as in the regulations and inspection framework within which they had to operate.[68]

In terms of actual teaching style, the most common criticism was insufficient differentiation.[69] Here differentiation means setting pupils different tasks according to their abilities. In some contexts, for example in closed-end maths activities, differentiation is most likely the most suitable option. However, although differentiation has become general practice across all lessons in the state sector, in many situations it is by no means the only appropriate approach. Instead of differentiation by activity, differentiation can also occur by outcome; providing pupils with the same tasks does not assume that they will all carry out the work at the same speed and level of detail and accuracy. Whilst there are benefits to differentiated activities, there are also benefits to be had from non-differentiation. For example, by not giving different sections of the class separate tasks, the class are unified in working towards a common goal. Moreover, although differentiated work can be beneficial by stretching the most able pupils with harder work, it is also too often used at the other end of the ability spectrum to 'baby-sit' pupils by keeping them occupied with simple tasks.

Pedagogically, differentiation is sold as more 'egalitarian' in that it offers pupils a greater chance to succeed in their work. However, differentiation could also be regarded as a form of streaming. Constantly segregating pupils by activity can lead to children being and feeling labelled according to their abilities, which for lower ability pupils poses the danger of keeping children at stagnant levels. Thus by no means is differentiation either the only teaching strategy available or always suitable. Indeed, in contexts where there do not tend to be huge disparities between pupils' learning levels, differentiation for the sake of differentiation can become superfluous. As with assessment, in state schools where large class size, wide ability spectra and discipline are greater issues, it could be argued that differentiation has been part of an attempt to combat these problems. This would therefore be another example of a response to a problem faced in state schools being imposed unnecessarily on the private sector to no purpose. That teaching can be effective without differentiation is something which OfSTED accepts—albeit inadvertently. In Dower House School's report teaching is described as 'good in two out of nearly every three lessons'.[70] Yet also at Dower House School 'few teachers plan explicitly for pupils of differing abilities'.[71] If differentiation is as fundamental to success as OfSTED suggests, these two judgements do not add up. This type of anomaly is widespread in OfSTED's reporting.

Non-differentiation relates to whole-class teaching, which was another area of criticism found in both the report and interview samples.[72] Pedagogical debate aside, this criticism is somewhat hypocritical as the issue of whole-class versus group work is one that the government has made more than one policy change on. In the early days of the National Literacy and Numeracy Strategies, for example, whole-class teaching was re-introduced, to subsequently fall out of fashion; then most recently it has been re-introduced again as a central lesson component (see Appendix 2: St George's).

A main problem of the regulations more generally is that many of them are based on what boils down to little more than opinion. The importance this government, and subsequently OfSTED, has attached to ICT illustrates this point. Half the schools across the samples were criticised for not giving ICT sufficient time in the curriculum, something the private sector has been repeatedly criticised for. In his 2003/2004 annual report, chief inspector David Bell argued that: 'despite having good resources, ICT is not used sufficiently in all subjects.'[73] There is, however, no evidence that the use of ICT is an effective learning tool, and recent research commissioned by OfSTED itself demonstrated the comparative ineffectiveness of computers for learning.[74]

> ***We don't have a problem with regulation* per se, *but when regulation moves into opinion.***
> *Kevin Avison, Steiner Waldorf Schools Fellowship, in interview*

Opinion-made-law applies not just to pedagogical matters but also to the more practical regulations. A pertinent example was given by West School. According to the DfES's regulations, all washbasins in pupil toilets must have running hot water.[75] Assuming that this requirement for hot water was for germ-killing purposes, West School instead provided all toilets with anti-bacterial soap. OfSTED refused to accept this alternative arrangement, and insisted that the school install hot water. When the school subsequently rang up the Department of Health they were told that this was not in fact a legal requirement under Health and Safety legislation; moreover they said that to kill germs water would have to be 60°c— although the DfES's regulations forbid water to be hotter than 43°c.[76] Nevertheless, OfSTED insisted that West School was bound by regulation and therefore law to install hot water and that failure to do so would mean failure to comply with requirements regarding 'the welfare, health and safety of the pupils'. Consequently as part of their action plan, West School has been forced to supply hot water.[77]

To illustrate the DfES/OfSTED discourse in the private sector, a school which did 'well' in inspection was compared with one that did 'badly'. This allowed for a comparison of what was praised in the school with the favourable report with what was criticised in the school with the unfavourable report. Thus the interviewed school which fulfilled all the requirements, West School, and the school which failed all but one requirement, South School, have been contrasted.

Both schools had full pupil rolls and consistently high records of academic achievement.[78] The schools' inspection reports have been dissected against background information from the interviews which allows an insight into how the two schools achieved their respective 'success' and 'failure'.

The successful school

Looking through West School's report, the recipe for success was clear: the school's education bore the closest resemblance to the state template, consequently fulfilling every regulation apart from 'the welfare health and safety of the pupils' (for not properly marking the attendance register). West School followed each of the nationally prescribed curricula: the Foundation Stage curriculum for the early years and all the National Curriculum core and foundation subjects, as well as Personal Social and Health Education (PSHE). All schemes of work were based on the National Curriculum and the school employed the Numeracy and Literacy Strategies. In addition, the school also put its pupils through both the Key Stage 1 and Key Stage 2 SATs and completed the national 'Foundation

Stage profiles' for pupils in the early years.

The school also mirrored much of the pedagogy currently used in the state sector, such as differentiation. In West School's report OfSTED praised highly the fact that the school matched work to pupils' abilities, giving more able pupils 'extended tasks'. That teachers made the 'learning objective' explicit to their pupils—required practice in the state sector—was also commended. Other state school initiatives used by the school such as 'circle time' were equally credited. OfSTED also commended the school's use of Individual Education Plans for pupils with special educational needs (SEN), which all SEN pupils are required to have in the state sector. In addition, West School fulfilled the majority of requirements regarding documented evidence. This included 'policy and procedure' related paperwork as well as paperwork for teaching purposes: planning and assessment. Much praise was given to the school's extensive documentation, especially when documents were 'detailed'. Each subject was described as having 'well defined' schemes of work and lessons were described as generally 'carefully' planned, taking into account pupil assessment. Recorded monitoring of progress was also frequently commented on: 'Pupils' progress is monitored rigorously throughout the school... the resulting information is carefully recorded'; 'records [of formal and informal test results] are kept to measure progress and to identify any gaps in knowledge'.[79]

The head teacher's dissection of the inspection outcomes illuminated both the process of achieving a good report and the reality behind the inspection judgements. What was particularly interesting about West School's case was that, although the school had done very well, the head teacher was very against much of the regulation and inspection process; in her view: 'the government is infringing on independent autonomy'. The head compared OfSTED's inspections of the independent sector with the previous system of HMI inspection, considering the latter as a considerably more interactive process than today's system of coming into schools purely to tick boxes. The head was keen to emphasise the enormous amount of preparation the school had done for the inspection. The majority of this preparation was carried out on the informal advice of the inspector, on her pre-inspection visit; the head teacher had also bought a piece of computer software designed to help independent schools through inspection. Much of the evidence which was so highly commended in the school's report, for example detailed lesson plans and assessment records, was generated purely for the purposes of inspection, regarded by the head as 'unnecessary' and 'unhelpful' for everyday teaching purposes. This once again demonstrates that, as well as emulating state school practices, temporarily creating the right 'inspection trail' plays a significant role in gaining a good OfSTED judgement.[80]

The unsuccessful school

South School received the least favourable report in the samples, failing in six out of the seven regulatory categories. Tellingly, out of all the schools sampled, South School's provision bore the least resemblance to state school arrangements. The school curriculum did not follow the design of the National Curriculum, nor any other DfES designed curricula, and did not put its pupils through any of the government-set tests.[81]

> ***The inspection framework could not accommodate a different type of school.***
>
> *South School*

The school was criticised on almost every single area of education-related provision: planning, teaching, assessment, documentary evidence and resources. Lessons were criticised for being 'over-directed' and for taking 'too little account of pupils' differing learning needs.' Planning was heavily criticised: for lack of detail on 'the methods and resources to be used'; for not indicating 'sufficiently how… differing needs and abilities' were to be catered for'; for not being informed by pupil assessment; and for 'inconsistencies'. The school was also criticised for not having schemes of work in place for each subject; and for lacking an 'effective framework' to 'assess and record pupils' progress'. Marking was another area which required 'development' as 'not enough is said about what pupils must do to improve'. Another weakness in need of being addressed was the fact that the school's reference books did not reflect the 'multiracial nature of society', re-iterated in the requirement 'the spiritual, moral, social and cultural development of pupils': 'more could be done to develop pupils' understanding of other cultures and lifestyles' (a criticism echoed in the rest of the reports). The school also performed poorly in relation to procedure and documentation of procedure in each other area of regulation apart from 'the spiritual, moral, social and cultural development of pupils'.

South School was very popular, and did very well academically, both in its pupils' performance in the 'Cognitive Abilities Tests' (CATs)[82] and in its successes in getting pupils into the selective secondary schools of their choice. In light of their successes, the school had decided not to be 'phased' by the inspection, and consequently did not carry out any preparation. The school described OfSTED's criticisms of the education it provided as being 'very unexpected'. South School felt that ultimately their provision had been penalised by being inspected according to a very 'limited' framework which was based on state arrangements—an accusation certainly supported by the evidence from the 'successful' school. Whilst the school was aware that it had weaknesses in its practical provision and some health and safety related areas—a new head teacher had only taken over three weeks before the inspection—these were regarded as mostly to do with the physical surroundings. The school's assumption had (wrongly) been that popularity and high levels of achievement would equate with a positive report on the education the school provided.[83]

A DfES template

> ***OfSTED measures schools according to state sector principles.***
> *Philip Bujak, Chief Executive of the Montessori Schools Association, in interview*

As illustrated by the comparison of West and South Schools, the independent sector is suddenly finding its provision measured against a standardised framework which not only fails to reflect its diversity, but actually *penalises* it for it. (Even West School, whose provision mirrored state arrangements so closely, was reprimanded for straying from precise directives such as not sufficiently delineating religious education and PSHE and not adhering one hundred per cent to the recommended style of marking.) The interviewees found the template their schools had been measured against to be destructively rigid. They felt that their schools had been judged unfairly, because they were not being measured in relation to the education they were providing but simply in relation to the pedagogy of the state sector. Moreover the respondents felt they increasingly had no choice but to homogenise their provision in line with this state model. West School, which fulfilled almost all the regulations, described the inspection process as 'trying to mould us, we had to fit the pattern and not continue as we were'.[84] South School's failure to comply with all but one regulation illustrated just how state-focused inspections are: 'Because we don't follow the National Curriculum, in lesson observations the inspectors didn't know what grade to give the lesson'. Similarly because the school did not do SATs 'the inspectors expressed uncertainty about what to write in their boxes'. (However, as we have seen, when schools do participate successfully in national testing, it is often unmentioned.)

Although schools fail regulation essentially on the grounds of not sufficiently emulating state practice, what was striking in the schools sampled was just how far their provision *did* echo that of the state sector. In the latest HMCI's annual report, the then Chief Inspector David Bell wrote that 'the quality of provision was higher in 2004/2005 than in the schools inspected last year'.[85] What Bell meant by this was that the number of private schools fulfilling the regulations was higher—as OfSTED equates getting schools to comply more stringently with government regulation as 'improving' them.[86]

> ***The Government respects the right of parents to choose an independent education for their children if they wish, and recognises that parents who chose to educate their children in an independent school may wish them to have a distinctive education which may not be readily available elsewhere.***
> *DfES, Independent Schools Information Sheet: 'What freedoms does the independent sector have?*

Since their introduction in 2003, the regulations for independent schools have become more entrenched. The more entrenched the requirements become, the more entrenched DfES methodologies become.

Although the implementation of the National Curriculum and SATs are not regulatory requirements, it has become clear to schools that success in inspection, and therefore ultimately public acclaim, is most easily achieved by mirroring state school arrangements. The irony, as one head teacher from the report sample commented: 'is that parents sending their children to independent schools are consciously trying to *avoid* state school arrangements—and making [financial] sacrifices to do so'.[87]

> ***The National Curriculum is not mandatory for independent schools but many schools follow it voluntarily.***
> *DfES, Independent Schools Information Sheet: 'Do schools have to teach the National Curriculum?'*

The worry is that this is the thin edge of the wedge. Once the inspection cycle is shortened from every six to every three years, more frequent enforcement of DfES pedagogy may lead to schools becoming less and less diverse.

Negating parent-power

The quasi-paternalistic, quasi-autocratic role of the state highlighted by Summerhill's case is also manifest in the

> ***The parents' response [to the unfavourable OfSTED report] was that [OfSTED] haven't shown the good aspects of the school.***
>
> *South School*

private school report and interview samples. Whilst it is perhaps more understandable (though no more legitimate) to fail a school on the basis of a policy of voluntary class attendance (as in Summerhill's case), it is totally unacceptable to do so on the grounds that a school is not employing aspects of teaching which are ultimately no more than a set of fluctuating pedagogical choices. The bottom line is that in neither case, regardless of one's own pedagogical perspective, should the state be entitled to intervene in the independent sector on issues further afield than basic health and safety.

Despite the DfES's increasingly common use of the buzzwords 'parental choice' and 'parent power' in relation to state schooling, the market mechanisms which genuinely enable these to be exercised in the private sector, whose very existence is based on parent power, are being impeded. Here parental choice is being negated as OfSTED enforces government-driven transformations in schools' ethos and curricula. Parents are *thwarted* from choosing the type of education they desire, as the school is thwarted from responding to market demands in the process of generating inspection information. It is in this context that a school in which OfSTED describes the parents as expressing 'a high level of satisfaction with the school' can receive a poor inspection report, failing over half of the government's regulations.[88]

Anthony Seldon is Master of Wellington College, a large association school. He is also a very high-profile supporter of private/state sector collaboration in education—and Tony Blair's biographer. In Dr Seldon's view, independence must necessarily work within a legal framework and therefore he sees it as entirely

> ***Independent schools have flourished in part because of their freedoms. Choking up this freedom with bureaucracy will atrophy this excellence.***
>
> *Dr Anthony Seldon, Master of Wellington College, in interview*

appropriate that private schools must comply with basic standards. However, Dr Seldon also considers the reason that the majority of private schools are excellent to be a result of market discipline: 'If schools are not performing they will go under because they'll lose their parents.'[89]

Similarly, all four interviewed schools regarded inspection of 'basic standards' to be vital, but the general feeling was that inspection should look only at provision relating to pupils' health and safety; one school suggested a trading standards type of inspection.[90] The schools were adamant that, in order to retain their independence: 'independent schools *must* be able to choose the way they run themselves'.[91] Current regulations were seen to be greatly at odds with this and 'infringing on private school autonomy'.[92] Regulation of education was not seen as legitimate. As one school commented: 'A school is as good or as bad as the number of parents who send their children to it—parents vote with their feet.'[93] Moreover, as well as passing judgement on aspects of a school which many would regard as outside its legitimate remit, OfSTED neglects to pronounce in areas where it could usefully cast some light. Considering the importance attached to value for money in the non-fee paying state sector (see chapter 2), the fact that there is no discussion whatsoever on the subject in private school reports is particularly noticeable. As independent schools work on a market basis, with considerable variation in the fees that they charge, a discussion of price in relation to facilities, for example, is something which might actually be helpful.

> ***Inspection of some sort is necessary to ensure basic standards, but not of the 'you will follow this trend' prescribed sort.***
>
> *West School*

However, returning to the purpose of inspection, the fact that value for money is only discussed in the state sector is not surprising as, where there is no government investment, there is no need to assure the taxpayer that public money is being monitored. 'Taxpayers should know how wisely their contribution to the substantial—and rising—education and care budget is being spent', OfSTED tells us.[94] OfSTED does not consider fee-paying parents to require such an evaluation of value for money.

The mechanism of parental choice is in danger: market value determined by popularity is being overtaken by the dominant orthodoxy of the OfSTED discourse. Central control is thwarting schools' ability to respond to the market by forcing them to respond to regulatory demands, whilst OfSTED's dominance over information supersedes the demands of parents. The result is a deeply unsatisfactory quasi-market in which market value is determined neither by objective criteria of excellence, nor by demand, but instead by the monopolisation of the definition of quality.

4
Who Inspects the Inspectors?

The Independent Schools Inspectorate (ISI)

> ***Schools are not measured against an arbitrary model [in ISI inspections] but against their own aims and goals.***
> *Durell Barnes, Head of Communications, ISI, in interview*

If the government is straitjacketing independent schools as described above, then why is it that the well established and highly influential Etons and Westminsters are not protesting? The predominant—although not the sole—reason is that the majority of 'well-known' schools are inspected by their own inspectorate, the Independent Schools Inspectorate (ISI), whose inspections are regarded as greatly preferable to OfSTED's inspection of the private sector. However, there are also other factors involved. Firstly, schools in membership of the Independent Schools Council tend to be both richer and larger than non-association schools, putting them in a better position to take the government's regulations in their stride. For example, a large staff means that the paperwork element of the regulations can be more easily accommodated.[1] The second factor is the current predominance of education in the political agenda: the government's appropriation and framing of education have made even the most powerful public schools surprisingly subservient to central doctrine.

Self-regulation

What makes the ISI's inspections preferable is that they present a truer and less restricted picture of schools. Although ISI-inspected schools are subject to exactly the same DfES regulations as OfSTED-inspected private schools, their inspections go 'above and beyond'.[2] (For this reason the Montessori Schools Association would also like to set up its own inspectorate in order to develop a less rigid inspection process for their schools.)[3] Thus the strengths and weaknesses of the school outside the regulations are recognised and reported on in ISI inspections. Furthermore, although former OfSTED inspectors often lead inspections, the inspection team is also made up of currently serving association school heads. This 'peer review' component of ISI inspection provides better protection against the straitjacketing dictation of what methodologies should be applied to the fulfilment of the regulations. Crucially this diffuses one of the key complaints about OfSTED's inspections of independent schools—being judged against the state school model. Thus, whilst evaluating a school's ethos and fulfilment of its own particular goals is *theoretically* part of OfSTED's own remit for private schools, ISI inspection arrangements actually realise this.

One outcome of the wider scope of ISI inspections is that the inspection process is much longer than that of OfSTED. The actual time the inspection team spend in schools is considerably longer, as is the time taken to prepare for inspection and the writing of the report. Ironically, OfSTED has distorted this benefit as a *disadvantage*, a reflection on the negative perception of OfSTED's inspections. In the document 'Inspection of Non-Association Independent Schools,' OfSTED describes its own fewer number of days spent on inspection as comparing 'favourably' with ISI inspections 'where inspection may take up to 70 inspector days'.[4] OfSTED's standard inspection of independent schools, in comparison, takes just 12 inspector days.[5] Although presumably cost is one of the factors OfSTED is alluding to, the other point of the comparison is the length of time and therefore level of detail in which a school is scrutinised. OfSTED is dismissing a key flaw in its own system: that a snapshot judgement restricted to regulatory requirements is actually far less beneficial for an

> ***We couldn't afford to join an association before—but we will now as it lessens the likelihood of being penalised for being unlike the state sector.***
>
> *South School*

independent school than a more detailed account of provision. Overall, rather than simply existing as exercises in enforcing compliance to regulation, ISI inspections are more constructive and collaborative processes.

In the current climate of central dominance in education the notion of safety in numbers particularly applies to the protection of the independent sector's freedoms. Being able to 'self-regulate' to an extent has been crucial to this. Inspection by the ISI instead of OfSTED is therefore a significant motivation for schools wanting to join an ISC association. Three out of the four schools that were interviewed for this report planned to join an association, their experiences of OfSTED very much a catalyst. However, membership of an association entails considerable expense, with ISI inspection costs on top. Moreover, many less well-off schools do not fulfil the criteria for membership, which again often relate to school finances, for example the fulfilment of teacher pay scales. West School, for example, which complied with almost all the DfES's regulations, had not joined an association because it could not afford the prerequisite teacher pay scales.[6] On the other hand, some schools have resisted association membership, not on account of expense but principle: in order to protect their autonomy.[7] However, with centralised control increasingly influencing autonomy in the private sector via mechanisms such as OfSTED inspection, surrendering some independence to association membership may be the better choice.

Freedoms with strings attached

> DfES regulation is affecting everyday practice in [private, ISC] schools.[8]

Although preferable to direct regulation by OfSTED, 'self-regulation', as the ISI refers to it, does not make the ISI immune from state control and all that is problematic about OfSTED's own inspections of the private sector. While it is 'professionally independent',[9] the ISI is under the supervision of both OfSTED and the DfES:

> ISI has been recognised by the Department for Education and Skills (DfES) and has been advising the government on the suitability of ISC schools for registration since 1999. From September 2003, ISI takes a further step and becomes a body approved for the purpose of inspection under Section (1)(b) of the Education Act 2002. A sample of our inspections are monitored by OfSTED.[10]

OfSTED's monitoring involves co-inspecting ten per cent of inspections, and evaluating 15 per cent of their reporting.[11] The ISI must comply with OfSTED's inspection regulations and address recommendations for improvement laid out in each annual review. Looking at the 'evolution' of ISI inspection, it is evident that the closer ISI inspections mirror OfSTED's own, the more positive their annual inspection report. Although it is the ISI's capacity to accommodate schools' idiosyncrasies which makes its inspections superior—something the newly introduced 'second cycle' arrangements have sought to heighten[12]—OfSTED's monitoring has simultaneously entailed a greater standardisation of procedure. Greater standardisation in inspection procedure has arguably entailed a greater level of standardisation in schools' provision. The standardisation of inspection procedure invariably leads to altering school practice to accommodate it. One example of this is judging pupil progress according to national benchmarks. In the 2003/04 ISI inspection report, OfSTED commented: 'although there have been improvements, there is inconsistent use of national comparative data when judging pupils' achievement.'[13] Their recommendation was that: 'training for team inspectors should continue to focus on… judging pupils' achievement and progress against national data'.[14] The following year, in the 2004/05 ISI inspection report, OfSTED commented that 'despite some improvement, this is still an area for continued development'.[15] The danger of requirement for such comparisons is that schools are pushed not just to adopt a greater emphasis on formal assessment, but also for primary level providers to implement national testing when they may not have chosen to otherwise (for example SATs). The adoption of national tests may in turn compel schools to implement the National Numeracy and Literacy Strategies (although evidence suggests that *not* doing so may in fact be better for performance). Another reported weakness in the 2003/04 ISI report was in judging pupil assessment procedures: the ISI was criticised for insufficient 'detail' in its 'reporting on the assessment of pupils'.[16] By the 2004/05 report OfSTED felt that this issue had been more or less addressed satisfactorily: 'Judgements about the effectiveness of assessment procedures are for the most part made explicitly'.[17] The requirement to present more detailed evidence of assessment procedures will again most likely entail schools having to provide both more standardised and a greater volume of documented evidence of assessment.

Thus, although this system of self-regulation is preferable, central intervention and therefore state-sector pedagogy still impact on school life. Yet association schools have expressed relatively little public criticism about this government control. It is unlikely that this is due to complete satisfaction. New Labour's emphasis on education has, in a variety of ways, put association schools in a somewhat deferential position. Centralised control over education has become such that government interference even in nominally independent activity is so much the norm that it is accepted. The interviewed association members and representatives' attitude to DfES regulation in ISI inspection illustrated this: there is a tangible element of gratefulness for the freedoms which the ISI have been granted by the DfES through self-regulation. This is a concerning indictment of the government's dominance over education: private sector freedoms should be a given, not an 'earned'[18] *privilege,* particularly when they are already limited. Yet the effect of central control means that rather than being up in arms over their curbed freedoms, the ISI and the associations are keen to keep OfSTED and the DfES happy. Increasingly fuzzy boundaries between educational provision and child protection have recently made it even more difficult

> ***I am proud that ISI is a trusted partner of the Department for Education and Skills.***
> *Tony Hubbard, former ISI Director, 2005*

to resist government intervention, with the inclusion of the inspection of social services into OfSTED's remit.

Another significant factor arguably keeping this section of the independent sector quietly complicit is their own involvement in their regulation. As large numbers of 'senior' teachers are also inspectors[19] in the ISI's system of peer review, they are less likely to be critical of OfSTED and the DfES; they are after all essentially working for OfSTED. This was apparent when talking to both head teachers involved in the inspections and various association officials. They were very wary about criticising OfSTED's role in the ISI—although inconsistently were perfectly prepared to be critical about every element of OfSTED's direct inspection of private schools. This last motivation to comply relates to two other contributing factors involving the ISI's former reputation and OfSTED's current reputation. While ISI was once accused of holding 'cosy' inspections, in the sense that inspection was performed internally and not regulated by an outside agency, OfSTED's role in ISI inspections today provides them with the necessary injection of apparent impartiality, and therefore validity.[20] As one association representative commented: 'OfSTED gives ISI inspections credibility'.[21] Indeed, although the ISI is keen to point out the superiority of its inspections in it publications, it is also keen to point out accreditation by OfSTED.[22]

The final contributing factor to the willing compliance of association schools with government policy is perhaps the most interesting as it most closely relates to the impact of New Labour education ideology. An education agenda based on benign goals of equality of opportunity has fostered a considerable amount of 'acceptable' anti-elitism. Question marks over their ethical worth in this agenda has led even top, seemingly 'untouchable' private schools to concede to central demands. This has been exacerbated by controversy over independent schools enjoying charitable status—although the Independent Schools Council is keen to point out that tax gains from their schools with charitable status are significantly outweighed by expenditure on scholarships and bursaries.[23] In 2004, almost £3 was given back, generally on fee assistance, for every £1 gained from charitable status.[24] In addition the private sector also saves the public purse around £2 billion.[25]

> ***Will the independent schools 'give something back' to the state sector? Yes, to defend their charitable status. The modernist thinking is about partnership, about private schools justifying their privileges by 'giving something back' to their communities.***
> *Andrew Adonis and Martin Bright, 1998*

Independent state partnership projects (ISPPs) are an illustration of the government's 'encouragement' for the independent sector to demonstrate its value to state education. Although this type of project is presented as 'sharing' between the sectors, more often than not they engage private schools in a non-reciprocal relationship with the state. For example, 90 per cent of all ISC schools now make at least one facility available for public use.[26] However, as the relationship between the sectors is theoretically also about the private sector learning from state schools, there is an even greater compulsion to take heed of state teaching methodologies. Former Chief Inspector David Bell echoed the government's calls for partnership between independent and state schools in the 2003 speech in which he denigrated sections of private school provision.[27] One of Bell's implications was that private schools could learn from their state counterparts—the addition of 'shamed disciplining' to social conscience as a compulsion to co-operate with the government's education strategies. This slant to the relationship between the private and the public sector has perhaps been intensified by the recent 'price-fixing' scandal, in which 50 of the ISC's top schools were found to be running an illegal fee-setting cartel.[28]

While the impact of the government's regulations may be mitigated in ISC schools, the question of legitimacy remains. Although association and ISI officials have pointed out in interviews that the ISI would have stipulated many of OfSTED's requirements independently, surely the rights and authority which the *government* has to make any such requirements should be questioned. The schools that are in the best position to protest against central intervention are those with a high level of gravitas on the grounds of their academic reputation and a loud lobbying voice thanks to their membership of a large umbrella organisation, and often significant affluence. Yet this is not happening. In October 2005, addressing the Headmasters' and Headmistresses' Conference, the broadcaster Libby Purves reprimanded the independent sector for being too afraid 'of becoming unpopular with the government' to join the national education debate. Continued cowardice will diminish what little debate there currently is even further.[29]

5
How Blair Became the School Bully

Under Thatcher, Major and Blair, greater dictation of schools' activities has been central to school improvement agendas. Although it is New Labour which has become synonymous with straitjacketing teachers, it was in fact the Conservatives' introduction of 'managerialist' techniques which set the ball of central intervention rolling. OfSTED, the National Curriculum and league tables were all the commanding tools of the Thatcher and Major governments. The powers over education granted in the 1988 Education Reform Act and subsequently are said to have made the 'Secretary of Education the envy of totalitarian regimes throughout the world'.[1]

For Blair, school improvement has been much more than a response to low standards. Education was the centrepiece of the election campaign which put him in power; it was the centrepiece of his democratic agenda and, above all, it was a personal mission: education was to be central to Blair's political legacy. Thus, no prime minister before Blair has invested so much politically, and further down the line financially, in education. As Smithers notes, whilst Blair thought the Thatcher and Major governments had been right to challenge education, he felt that they had failed to support schools in the improvement drive.[2] Blair planned to rectify this by providing that missing support: support which would translate into control. Thus, the unprecedented elevation of the stakes in the school improvement drive would also entail an unprecedented level of government intervention in schools.

A pledge to raise the education system from third-rate to 'world class'[3] was the perfect ideological and political vehicle for a re-branded Labour party. New Labour's promise to transform the education system demonstrated its continued commitment to a social democratic agenda, whilst simultaneously extricating itself from the utopian 'old' Labour principles of un-won entitlement. Blair's vision of social democracy was a departure from egalitarianism towards *meritocratic* equality of opportunity.[4]

> ***I believe in a country where hard work and merit, not privilege or background, determine success.***
>
> *Tony Blair, general election campaign speech, 2005*

In other words, Blair's vision was a more conservative one, concerned with the redistribution of life chances rather than the redistribution of wealth. Nevertheless, Blair's plans for the social and economic engineering capacity of education were highly idealistic. Excellent schools would foster a more equal society by removing class as an obstacle to opportunity—creating a workforce able to compete in the global economy to boot. These plans for education were ambitious to say the least.

> ***If I had to characterise the Blair government's approach to education, I would say that it has desperately wanted to be seen to be doing good things. Every day without a new education headline was regarded as a day wasted...***
>
> *Professor Alan Smithers, director of the Centre for Education and Employment Research Buckingham University, 2001*

Certainly, over the last nine years, the New Labour government has been very active in education. However, constant activity has not always equated with progress; indeed, all too frequently, quite the reverse. Whilst there has been improvement in quantifiable standards, its validity has frequently been questioned. Furthermore, any improvement that has been made has arguably been outweighed by the damaging effects of government policy on the 'infrastructure' of the education system.

The New Labour government set itself test goals to measure how effectively they were driving improvement.[5] Its fixation with improvement thus became a fixation with targets. Armed with confidence and a desire to demonstrate ambition, the government launched its initial reforms with overly optimistic targets: targets, described

> ***The priority should be children's literacy and not the prime minister's legacy.***
>
> *Edward Davey, former Liberal Democrat education spokesperson, 2003*

by the NUT as 'plucked out of thin air',[6] which would come to haunt the government and schools. Many of the targets labelled 'bold' and 'determined' at the time might have been better described as unrealistic—as in the case of those set for the primary sector. Here the emphasis was on literacy and numeracy, taught in the Literacy and Numeracy Hours. The targets which accompanied the introduction of the Literacy and Numeracy Strategies, in 1998 and 1999 respectively, pledged that the number of primary school leavers (Year 6) achieving Level 4 in literacy and numeracy SATs would rise to 80 per cent (from the 1995 level of 44 per cent) and 75 per cent (from 48 per cent) respectively by 2002.[7] These targets were not met.[8] Smithers suggests that one reason for not reaching them was that the government had perhaps misunderstood quite how ambitious they were.[9] Under the Conservatives Level 4 was set as the *average* level of attainment, meaning that roughly 50 per cent could be expected to reach or exceed it. New Labour, however, took Level 4 as the *expected* level, i.e. a level achievable by every Year 6 pupil. What had been targets were reframed as standards. Perhaps this effort to defy the normal distribution of ability was deliberate; something Blair's equalising agenda was striving for (although it would be reverting to an equality closer to old Labour egalitarianism).

The practicalities of attaining these levels of achievement have, however, proved rather more difficult than making the promises. As a result, reported primary level improvement cannot always be taken at face value, often signifying teaching to the test rather than the narrowing of the achievement gap. Thus, although the 2002 targets were missed, as were subsequent ones, there has been quantifiable progress in primary test performance. The 2002 target for numeracy was finally hit three years late, in 2005, and the 2002 literacy target only narrowly missed.[10] (However, whilst SATs results were better than in 2004 in 53 per cent of primary schools in 2005, they were *worse* in 45 per cent of schools.)[11] The new problem is the targets set for 2006—85 per cent for both numeracy and literacy—which again look unreachable. Yet the government adamantly maintains that their 2006 target will be reached.[12]

The value of SATs performance has already been widely questioned by educationalists: what does the progress actually measure? As well as evidence of lower pass marks in the national tests,[13] alternative measures of achievement such as those of Durham University's Curriculum, Evaluation and Management Centre (CEM) have found that increases in test results, particularly in literacy, were more to do with test preparation than they were to do with rises in actual learning levels.[14] In their own independent tests, which have been carried out annually since 1997 on 5,000 children across 120 schools, CEM has found no evidence of a rise in literacy levels.[15] Research from St Martin's College, Lancaster has also found primary improvement to have been overstated.[16]

The Audit Commission has warned this government about its dangerous obsession with setting and reaching benchmarks. In 2003 the commission argued that targets frequently led to 'perverse consequences' whereby public sector employees were 'gamed' to meet targets while failing to genuinely improve performance.[17] OfSTED however has not shown similar concern, all too often pointing to rising test scores as evidence of successful strategy.[18] Teaching to the test is a problem, not just because of the misleading outcomes, but also because of the insecurities it leaves in pupils' knowledge. In other words, performance in relation to targets not only does not guarantee actual improvement, it may also potentially lower it. SATs preparation runs the risk of sacrificing learning for targets, and indeed there has been serious concern about primary school leavers being unable to cope with the secondary curriculum.[19] In this sense the government's determination for a test performance jump from 75 per cent to 85 per cent in numeracy and 79 per cent to 85 per cent in literacy in one year becomes far more worrying for learning standards than for the possibility of the missed targets. In 2004 the QCA found that 75 per cent of year 6 classes were spending a tenth of all teaching time practicing for the literacy SATs—from as early on as halfway through the autumn term.[20] Mounting pressure to reach the 2006 target is likely to have increased test preparation time even more.

On the other hand, similar numeracy tests carried out by CEM did find evidence of improvement. However, as Professor Peter Tymms, Director of CEM points out: 'it is easier to impact on maths.'[21] Nevertheless, methodologies in the Numeracy Strategy have also been criticised, particularly calculation techniques, regarded as 'Victorian' by some and simply confusing by others.[22] The government's desire to innovate has meant the implementation of often overly complicated hallmark New Labour methods. Although the espoused aim of the Numeracy and Literacy Strategies was a 'back to basics' approach,[23] the outcome has frequently been a case of reinventing the wheel with unnecessarily complicated results.

The greatest problem with the Literacy and Numeracy Hours, prescriptive down to five-minute intervals, is the coupling of inflexible dictation of teaching methods with the rigid dictation of what must be covered. Research by Hargreaves *et al.*, published in the *Cambridge Journal of Education* in 2002, found that the need to 'cover the ground' in the Literacy Hour was hampering pupils' thinking and speaking development:[24]

> In an educational climate dominated by monitoring, inspection and test results, teaching for understanding was regarded as an optional extra, permissible once the learning objectives had been met.[25]

Hargreaves *et al.*'s findings are unsurprising considering that, for example, in the National Literacy Strategy: 'the teacher is not supposed to divert from the lesson's stated objectives, however interesting a child's remark'.[26]

Now that it has become impossible to disregard the evidence any longer, the government is finally bringing back synthetic phonics as a central strategy for teaching reading. However, the point is not about pedagogy but rather about the fact that former Education Secretary Ruth Kelly announced in December 2005 that it would now become 'statutory' for every maintained school in the country to teach reading via synthetic phonics. Despite nearly ten years worth of evidence on the damaging effects of restricting teachers, the government is clearly not planning to loosen its grip on school activity.

Governmental control over the minutiae of education stretches far further than numeracy and literacy in the primary sector. In 2004 the Conservative party produced research demonstrating the sheer volume of central control over schools generally. The so-called *Red Tape* report calculated that more targets and criteria were set for schools by Whitehall than there were days in the school year.[27]

Failure to deliver the type of transformation promised has meant the government finding itself repeatedly faced with the same dilemma: acknowledging systemic flaws and losing credibility over strategies, or storming on. What has been an imperious rolling out of initiatives, which have forced schools to teach in specific ways with specific materials, has made admission of defective methods very difficult politically. This has led to the development of a vicious circle of greater intervention as damage control for previous intervention, creating a level of central interference in schools more akin to dictatorship than democracy. The effect has been one of what Labour MP David Chaytor described as 'a policy of permanent revolution'.[28] This restless cycle has however been publicly presented as a positive: a perpetual 'improvement drive' where continual change is a pre-requisite. Challenging continuous change and proposing

> ***Over the last eight years we have launched a series of bewildering initiatives in quick succession—often without evaluating the success of one before moving on to the next.***
> *David Chaytor MP, 2006*

instead forms of consolidation has perversely come to be labelled as irresponsible complacency.

For teachers, the government's improvement initiatives have frequently been alienating, with serious staff shortages as a result. The government has sought to tackle ensuing recruitment and retention problems via financial incentives, yet where dissatisfaction persists it is around non-pecuniary issues. New Labour's reforms have heavily increased teachers' administrative duties, as they have required much documenting of procedure. Chevalier and Dolton have found that graduate teachers are 12 percentage points more likely to be dissatisfied with their hours than other graduates,[29] with evidence from Smithers and Robinson showing that workload ranks significantly higher than pay in reasons for teachers quitting the profession.[30] In fairness, the government *has* responded, albeit rather late, to complaints over the bureaucratic burden faced by schools. In January 2004 the government introduced the 'New Relationship with Schools' initiative, with the reduction of paperwork a central aim.[31] Nevertheless, over a year later in 2005 the National Foundation for Educational Research found in an evaluation of the initiative's impact that teachers detected little change.[32] As well as alienating teachers through workload, the regulatory burden has also caused resentment in relation to their professionalism. Administrative duties denote the government's control over teachers' activities—interpreted as 'mistrust'. A recent study of 50 primary schools from the University of York found that current education policies were '...viewed [by teachers] as an expression of the government's lack of trust in the teaching profession—which... lowered morale and reduced teacher self-confidence'.[33]

In short, a benign, even admirable goal of rapidly improving the education system has turned Blair into the school bully, responsible for stalling progress and wasting money in the state sector as well as thwarting autonomy and wasting money in the private sector. Government policy has become dictatorial to the extent that even the

> ***The concentration of decision-making at the centre has led to a situation where 'command and control' dominates, and this has now reached a point where it is seriously counter-productive.***
>
> *Sir John Cassells, director of the National Commission on Education, 2003*

private, theoretically immune sector, now has to adhere to centrally imposed regulation. In state schools, teachers' input and output is policed from the vocabulary they write on the board and how they divide up their lessons to the exact progress their pupils must make. In private schools, teachers must heed the pedagogic fashions of the DfES, making concessions in their own methodologies and documenting their actions for unnecessary approval.

Underlying Blair's school improvement agenda was a newly formulated class battle. Education was to be the equalising instrument. Socio-economic barriers would fall away at the school gates, the classroom becoming a melting pot producing a solution of equality in excellence. Within the equalising rhetoric, the private sector became something of a sacrificial lamb. The stark disparity in performance between the two sectors was a grating reminder of the relationship between class and achievement, wholly at odds with the equality of opportunity that Blair was espousing. Thus, not only would the improvement drive close this achievement gap, as Blair's biographer Anthony Seldon put it, the Prime Minister's vision was that 'state schooling would improve so much that the independent school would wither on its vine'.[34]

> ***For generations our country has been held back by an education system that excelled for the privileged few but let down the majority.***
>
> *Labour Party Manifesto, 2005*

But this has not been the case. Nearly ten years on, Blair's reforms have not simply failed to remove the thorn, the private sector, in the side of the state education system, they have forced it further in. Rather than eliminating the need for an alternative sector, the policies intended to do so have conversely *compelled* parents and teachers to enter into it. A new demand for low-fee schools, catering for a clientele new to the independent sector, has sprung-up as a direct response to poor state provision. These schools are frequently run by teachers disenchanted with the over-regulation of the state sector, and patronised by parents let down by poor provision.

In an ironic full circle it is these small schools (which tend not to be rich enough to be association members) which are finding themselves penalised by OfSTED inspection. Thus, whilst the demand for an alternative to state provision has increased, government regulation is making it very difficult for alternative forms of provision to survive. Compounding the irony, the survival of these schools frequently set up as an antidote to poor quality in the state sector is jeopardised by their failure to comply with state school 'quality'. As a climactic irony, in a context where OfSTED judgment dictates quality, parents who are consciously avoiding state methodologies find themselves picking independent schools which have good inspection judgments and therefore bear a closer resemblance to state school provision.

Alternative, private methods, are sabotaging Blair's vision for the state education sector, both in theory and in practice. The government has taken control of the minutiae in state schools with the legitimising principle that New Labour pedagogy is the best choice, and is therefore the only way to raise standards. However, the private sector's deviance from government pedagogy, together with its consistently higher performance, seriously undermines the legitimacy of the government's control over schools. The government has reacted to this by undermining both the power and performance of the private sector, by granting itself the authority to regulate independent schools. The ostensible purpose of private sector regulation is consumer protection. However, we have seen that regulation goes far beyond protecting the health and safety concerns of the consumer, extending to heavy-handed regulation of the quality of education. The regulation judges schools according to DfES pedagogy, so that at the same time as asserting the value of this pedagogy it attacks alternative pedagogies.

OfSTED has been the vehicle enabling the level of control necessary to dictate the behaviour of schools. OfSTED inspects 'quality' of education and ensures corresponding processes of 'improvement', their definitions determined, though constantly changing, by the DfES. It is this *monopoly* on what counts as 'good' that is responsible for the penalising and straitjacketing of the independent sector. A powerful network of managerialist[35] principles and distrust in the professionalism of teachers, instigated by Conservative governments but magnified by New Labour, have been organised into an Orwellian system of what Rose refers to as 'governing at a distance'.

Managerialism

> ***The school system has become 'industrial', with industrialised quality control and an industrialised regulatory regime.***
> *Alan Gotch, Association of Teachers and Lecturers' representative in interview*

The re-organisation of the public services according to market principles can be traced back to the Conservative policies of the 1980s.[36] Efforts to make efficiencies in public spending were led by Conservative assertions of the 'innate superiority of the market over the state' and the overarching desire to withdraw from Keynesian welfarism.[37] The 1980s managerial structural model became a template for achieving 'organisational excellence'.[38] As education standards became an increasing political concern for the Thatcher government (relating to the perceived risks of competition amid growing globalisation),[39] managerialist principles of organisational excellence were particularly impressed upon schools. Attempts to achieve this notion of efficiency and excellence led to a string of education policies which increased control over the day-to-day running of schools. Central to this appropriation of control was the introduction of a National Curriculum, brought in under the 1988 Education Act and designed to combat irregularities in teaching quality. John Major continued the commandeering of teachers by introducing the publication of league tables, target-setting and the foundation of OfSTED, all in 1992.[40] The standardisation of what was taught and what was measured was intended to allow schools to function in a competitive market by enabling comparability.[41]

> ***In specifying its requirements so precisely, the government crossed the line between telling schools what to teach and telling them how to teach.***
> *Professor Alan Smithers discussing the Numeracy and Literacy Strategies, 2001*

More than two decades on, and within a brand new ideology, managerialist principles of efficiency and excellence have not just persisted but have been significantly inflated. Quality and excellence have become very much New Labour 'hurrah' words, as Smyth and Shacklock put it.[42] Whilst old Labour would most likely have rejected and dismantled the managerialist organisation of the public services, the party's rebirth as 'New Labour' has involved adopting many of the premises of neo-liberalism in the public services.[43] In education, New Labour has consistently intensified managerialism over its three terms in power, coupling heightened intervention with the ubiquitous target. Apparently as keen as the Conservatives to dismantle the role of the LEA in schools, Blair has more or less discarded its job as the advisory middleman, reframing it instead as a cog in the mechanism of central control. The Blair government has coupled 'command' policies inherited from the Conservatives with its own 'control' policies. This has entailed a series of interventions, most significantly the introduction of the Literacy and Numeracy Strategies in the early days of New Labour power (1998 and 1999), and more recently a statutory curriculum for infants from birth to three (2005).[44]

Rhetorically, this managerialism has evolved. The focus has been lifted from a customer-service and taxpayer focus on the benefits of the market to one of more accountability in the pursuit of greater democracy.[45] The New Labour assumption has been that strategies of performance-oriented managerialism can be harnessed unproblematically to a social democratic agenda concerned with promoting social inclusion and equality.[46] The underlying market-force principles persist: value for money, customer satisfaction, continuous improvement and productivity. This is omnipresent language in the public services, especially education.[47] What distinguishes—and particularly problematises—New Labour's adoption of the 'organisational excellence' template is the way it has been awkwardly merged with a far greater emphasis on state-centred regulation. Whilst the Conservatives saw regulatory bureaucracy as deeply cumbersome and the dynamism of competition achievable only in the unfettered market, New Labour has incorporated managerialist techniques into a highly bureaucratic framework.[48] Thus, while continuing the Conservative drive to restructure schools according to competitive market principles, Blair has disabled genuine competition with regulation. Managerialism for the Conservatives involved dictating what subjects were taught in order to pit schools against each other in testing. Managerialism for New Labour has meant adding *how* to teach and how to assess into the equation. Doing so has prevented schools from competing freely, as compliance replaces innovation. As the Conservative legacy of pupil-led funding continues, schools have become straitjacketed in how they compete for custom. The bottom line for schools is responsibility without power.[49] Hoggett refers to this mishmash of marketisation and regulation as a 'mongrel' model of governance.[50] The difficulty with this hybrid is that the rigidity and predictability of bureaucracy are very much at odds with the flexibility and innovation that the market requires.

Such a 'mongrel' model of governance very much echoes Giddens' 'Third Way' vision (although he would doubtless prefer the term 'crossbreed' himself). The Third

Way has played an enormous role in determining the shape of Blair's public services, seeking to achieve 'a new political position between neo-liberalism and social democracy which is seen to transcend both'.[51] Giddens' thesis argues for 'a synergy between public and private sectors', asserting the desirability of 'a balance between regulation and deregulation'.[52] His proposed 'mixed economy' combines market-based solutions with 'administrative efficiency' (including regulatory mechanisms)[53]—strikingly akin to the organisation of contemporary education policy. Giddens believes that governments '...have a lot to learn from business "best practice", such as target controls, effective auditing, accountability and efficiency'.[54] Summing up the Third Way vision, Giddens argues that this regulated public sector ultimately requires the impetus of 'market discipline'.[55] The coupling of 'market' with 'discipline' perfectly captures the paradoxical state of current education: the new emphasis on the role of the parent and taxpayer as customers claiming to induce competition, quality and efficiency into the system ('market'), with 'discipline' capturing its regulatory nature. Schools are not allowed to be genuinely competitive, and therefore the application of managerialist principles cannot be organic in any way. In the private sector, where schools are genuinely functioning in a market, the government's 'discipline' in the form of statutory regulation is thwarting their ability to respond to it—coupled with OfSTED dominance distorting the market itself. What ensures that schools do, therefore, comply with managerialist policy are bureaucratic arrangements which are both enabled by and themselves enable surveillance.

Bureaucracy

New Labour has shackled managerialist principles with a tight regulatory framework. The result is that schools are given a false sense of competition and autonomy, whilst in fact they have virtually no decision-making power. This power has been removed from schools as the government

> ***In our first term, we transformed recruitment, training and methods of teaching.***
> *Labour Party Manifesto 2005*

has appropriated control over school activity. This has been achieved through a powerful network whereby initiatives are enshrined in law, these laws are spread through bureaucratic channels and then enforced through audit.

The current organisation of the education system, with teachers making up the bottom layer of a pyramid-shaped structure of power, their actions dictated by rule-abiding officials, resonates strongly with Max Weber's typology of the bureaucracy. All action is dictated by rules disseminated through documentation and rule-abiding officials: it is estimated that the DfES issues schools with approximately 12 pages of directives a day.[56] Weber describes this 'bureaucracy' as the optimum way of 'organising large numbers of people effectively',[57] distinguishable from other systems of organisation by its 'explicit design in the shaping of its activities and goals'.[58] Bureaucratic rule therefore presents an excellent method of controlling the daily activities of a nation's teaching force. Moreover, bureaucratic arrangements hold enormous appeal for a government which seeks this level of control, but does not wish to appear authoritarian.[59] This fits with New Labour's claim of having discarded ideology in education and thereby de-politicised its policies in favour of pragmatism.[60] Political decisions are transformed into technical ones, what Habermas refers to as the 'scientifization of politics'.[61] Goal and activity control is sold in neutralised, scientific, rational terms. This is possible as dictation exercised through the bureaucracy is not perceived as insidious, but instead as faceless and dull. Comparatively unobtrusive application of regulation in schools has standardised school activity and removed 'whim'.[62] By definition, the bureaucracy limits initiative, ensuring that decisions are taken according to specific criteria rather than individual choice.[63]

Weber expands on this idea of eradicating initiative by arguing that bureaucratic organisation necessarily involves cutting out the 'talented amateur', ensuring instead a general level of competence.[64] In schools most action is determined by the DfES and thus independent agency is constrained. A compliant and predictable workforce is fundamental to a goal of controlling activity with the aim of controlling outcomes. Here the 'talented amateur' is not an asset. Instead, as Weber explains, workers are trained to become 'experts' in the system.[65] The nature of teacher training, in-school teacher training (INSET) and ongoing DfES directives for schools, have created a generation of system experts, experts in New Labour's educational bureaucracy. Graduate recruitment into teaching has risen by 70 per cent since 1997.[66] The year-long Post-Graduate Certificate in Education (PGCE) focuses almost entirely on training students in DfES policy. The sheer volume of DfES diktat together with the relatively short training period leaves little time for comparative pedagogy. With little thought therefore fostered 'outside the DfES box', the new generation of experts come to know nothing better or worse than the methodologies espoused by the DfES. Hill describes teacher education under New Labour as 'increasingly regulated, technicist and de-theorised'.[67] The very low retention rate of teachers[68] means a constant need for new recruits, and therefore new trainees. There is consequently a continuous influx of newly trained 'experts' entering the system, rapidly subsuming the declining number of teachers not trained under New Labour. That teachers are becoming 'better' at OfSTED inspection is therefore of little surprise. A recent OfSTED survey showed that recently trained teachers scored twice as well in inspection compared with older teachers trained in a different system.[69] Similarly, OfSTED research shows that 'good teaching' in primary schools rose from 45 per

> ***[S]chools must be granted more autonomy: but in a one dimensional paradigm where education is about quantifiable results this discussion is not being had.***
> *Alan Gotch, Association of Teachers and Lecturers' representative in interview*

cent in 1997 to 74 per cent in 2004,[70] and in 2003 OfSTED declared newly qualified teachers trained under the current OfSTED-monitored teacher training regime as the best-ever trained.[71] OfSTED inspectors have also become experts in the system, now divested of any professional judgement and discretion and under strict direction to follow a rigid framework. The inspectors' role now revolves around mechanically ticking boxes, their purpose being to standardise the behaviour of teachers according to desired norms and outcomes. With the new experts flooding the system and the tentacles of the bureaucracy now reaching into the independent sector, private school teachers, not trained in DfES dogma, find their professionalism undermined. They are not experts in the educational bureaucracy, therefore they are no longer considered education experts:

> Accumulated wisdom acquired through many years of successful classroom teaching was denigrated because it did not equate with the skill requirements embodied in the criteria... the ability to mouth the rhetoric, and systemic policy.[72]

In light of these notions of mechanical expertise and the production-line nature of teacher training today, the government's teacher training recruitment campaign is ironic. Their advertisements depict office workers as headless, implying that teaching is more stimulating with far greater potential for creativity. *'Use your head'*, the advertisement tells us, *'teach'*. The additional irony is that had teaching not become as robotic and restrictive as it has, there probably would have been no need for the recruitment campaign at all. With paperwork a key reason for low retention rates in teaching, former teachers are heading back to the less bureaucratic office. (Or to become cleaners as in the recent case of two teachers who, disillusioned by the workload, have left teaching to set up a cleaning business—a story received in the education press not with incredulity but with worrying understanding.)[73]

The recruitment crisis to which this campaign is responding resonates with another element of Weber's bureaucratic typology. Whilst those higher up the bureaucratic hierarchy regard their jobs as continuous 'careers', the bottom layer of the organisation is considerably less stable.[74] This is increasingly the case for the largest but least powerful layer of the educational hierarchy as teaching becomes more de-professionalised and more transient. Today's short retention span in teaching recalls another element in Weber's typology, namely the lack of ownership of the workers' resources. Central dictation of school activity has led to a rapid decline in teacher-ownership of pedagogic resources. Teaching resources, materials, plans, and curricula are increasingly centrally prescribed, extending also to intellectual resources as teachers are forced to become more and more robotic.

Audit and surveillance

Bureaucratic arrangements provide only the regulatory channels for central control; on their own these cannot guarantee enforcement. Compliance with regulation requires mechanisms which compel teachers to standardise their behaviour according to the desired norms. Michel Foucault describes the enforcement of the 'normative order' as hinging on a combination of discreet and indiscreet forms of power. Understanding how these forms of power come about and function is particularly important to understanding the position in which the OfSTED-inspected private school now finds itself. A sector theoretically immune from government control is silently complying with DfES dogma. What could be termed 'coercive accountability' is preventing private schools from being able to resist the government's infringement on their freedoms.

In the same way that managerialism has been borrowed from business and applied to education, another form of 'conceptual migration' in education is the application of audit.[75] Power describes audit as a risk reduction technology which inhibits deviant actions.[76] Those successfully audited demonstrate their non-deviance and thereby their trustworthiness within the system: in audit-speak this makes them accountable. The power of audit in education lies in the repercussions of not attaining this accountability. When an agency such as OfSTED has a monopoly over audit, therefore, it also has a monopoly over granting accountability. As we have seen, this makes the agenda to which the auditing agency is working fundamentally important.

Audit in the form of OfSTED has had extreme consequences for the state education system; in the name of regulating standards in schools OfSTED has effectively achieved a homogenisation of teaching. The risk of non-compliant teachers has been reduced as audit has minimised deviance by regular monitoring. A network of managerialism, bureaucracy and audit compels schools to demonstrate their compliance to regulation in order to fulfil the required goals.

Whilst audit is concerned with ascertaining and producing accountability and trust, it can also be seen as a technology of *mistrust*.[77] Centring on the idea that unmonitored activity is inherently worrying, outsiders are summoned to restore trust by scrutiny and discipline.[78] This is very much the approach adopted by OfSTED, where a distrust of teachers is coupled with draconian testing and disciplining. OfSTED's power lies in its guise of both tackling a mistrust of teachers and tackling public mistrust of political involvement in education. However, OfSTED's relationship with the DfES means that far from being protected against it, pupils are veritably exposed to an untrustworthiness of both teachers and politicians. OfSTED enforces a politicised agenda and teachers fabricate in order to conform to it. Public perception sees the auditory relationship of power between scrutiniser and observed as between OfSTED and schools, not, as it is in reality, between the DfES and schools. This leads to the perverse situation where public outcry against low standards, a result of DfES policy, entails the further entrenchment of government policy as OfSTED ups its game by 'raising the bar'. Raising the bar means upping levels of compliance.

OfSTED's regular check-ups on schools' input and output are most directly responsible for implementing the political education agenda. With the private sector now included in OfSTED's remit, the homogenising impact of government regulation is creeping also into independent schools. The inspectorate's surveillance mechanisms provide the catalytic impetus to compel schools to comply with government policy. Foucault's writings on methods of discipline illuminate these mechanisms which have granted the government omnipotence in education. The disciplining of the teacher and independent proprietor involve a combination of physical and documentary surveillance through a dispersal of power and intimidation, both imposed and internalised.

Since the coupling of OfSTED inspection with escalated regulation of school activity, what Rose refers to as 'techniques of government'[79] have created more accountable, and thereby more controlled schools. These 'techniques' include requiring people to write things down and checking that they have done so. The large quantity of paperwork entailed in OfSTED's inspections demonstrates the application of regulation to teaching. Now that private schools are also subject to DfES regulation, they are finding themselves having to document activity on an unprecedented level.

Most significant in relation to the curbing of the freedoms in the independent sector is the definition of quality. Quality has become defined in auditable terms[80], thereby standardised according to the pedagogical orthodoxy of the time: the government's. If provision does not fit the monopolising criteria then it cannot be of satisfactory quality.[81] The educator becomes reduced to an 'inspectorable template', forced to reorganise to accommodate accountability mechanisms[82]. In the private sector this has entailed adopting the National Curriculum and participating in SATs.

External subjection is only half of the disciplining equation. Supplementary to external subjection is 'internal subjectification':[83] self-regulation. Once the individual is self-regulating, the normative order becomes far more powerful than it would do through indiscreet coercion alone.[84] Self-regulation has become particularly pervasive in the state sector with the inclusion of 'self-evaluation'—a benign misnomer for the most insidious mechanism in the school inspection process to date. Self-evaluation has exactly *not* been about placing 'trust in a school's own assessment of its strengths', as former schools' minister David Miliband claimed, but rather about making schools regulate themselves.[85]

The compulsion to comply is bound up in the fear of resistance and criticism relating to the high-stakes nature of OfSTED reporting, together with the imperative nature of accountability in a context involving children. Disagreeing with the one body in education through which accountability is obtainable jeopardises a school's public reputation. 'Resistance to accountability—that's the suspicion when teachers are critical of OfSTED, and explains why schools aren't more vocal', commented a union representative, who did not want to be named.[86] The powerful coupling of the necessity for a school to be publicly accountable with the sole way to achieve that accountability inextricably tied up in the DfES's monopoly of the definition of quality, means that criticism of OfSTED is not simply futile but potentially self-harming. The DfES's input into OfSTED's auditing activity therefore means that schools which do not comply with the government's requirements become untrustworthy. Thus, despite widespread ideological resistance to policy on the part of both the state and the private sector, what become 'technologies of the self'[87] ensure their ongoing participation in its perpetuation. This allows OfSTED to be able to declare that 'complaints about inspection are very rare'.[88]

The force of OfSTED's public image creates an additional source of self-regulation as the inspectorate dominates the production of information about schools. As we have seen, private schools have become particularly susceptible to the powers of this 'information'. Justifying OfSTED's intervention into the independent sector, former HMCI David Bell argued that for the private education market to function well there needs to be information on schools in the public domain: 'To work effectively a market needs reliable and easily available information'.[89] The caveat here is that the source of this information determines the content of it. Here the reference is to OfSTED reporting, 'information' which conforms to a very particular agenda and therefore distorts rather than facilitates true market mechanisms. As O'Neill comments, one must not confuse communication, which often has a purpose, with neutral information.[90] This distortion of the market affects both provider and consumer as allegedly empowering information is in fact *disempowering.* Consumers find themselves acting not out of personal choice but political coercion. The way in which the dominant orthodoxy of OfSTED reporting subsumes the concept of information on schools in the private sector has therefore perverted parental decision-making. Parents find themselves compelled to become dissatisfied with schools they had previously been very happy with because of information received from OfSTED.

> ***Performance tables and inspections have given many parents the information that has enabled them to make objective judgements.***
>
> *Tony Blair, Foreword to the 2005 Education White Paper*

Recent amendments to education acts and inspection frameworks relate very closely to the concept of risk in modern society. Insecurities of every kind have become subject to risk management strategies,[91] highlighting potential risk. The concept of risk has been vital to the government's appropriation of control over the activities of teachers, pupils and parents: the risk of irresponsible teaching, of pupils not prepared for tomorrow's economy, of uninformed parents. In the independent sector, risk is asserted via increased regulatory requirements to do with health and safety, CRB clearance (child protection) and complaints channels (consumer protection). The 'suitability of the staff and proprietor' and 'the effectiveness of the school's procedure for handling complaints' are central tenets of OfSTED's legitimacy to intervene in the independent private sector. Subsequently, intervention in the form of inspection is legitimised as reassuring parents that educators, via experts (OfSTED inspectors), are minimising risks. Yet in practice these areas of regulation pale in comparison to OfSTED's scrutiny of educational provision. More recently formulated 'security' risks have helped legitimise the intervention of the state into what is actually taught in private schools. An increasingly cited justification for inspecting more than basic health and safety standards in the independent sector is that educational provision must be regulated to protect against the teaching of religious fundamentalism. The non-compliant teacher who does not adhere to OfSTED regulations can therefore be publicly declared as untrustworthy and irresponsible. This returns to the idea of mistrust, a central component of panopticon-style governmental surveillance: in the midst of this normative monopoly the unregulated are deemed unlikely to be providing a satisfactory education. In this sense the government's strong hold over the independent sector has come very naturally.

However, because the model of surveillance is not perfect, with compliance to regulation not constantly enforced, there is room for malfunction within the system as teachers revert to their own devices whilst unwatched. (Self-evaluation is, however, contributing to a more truly panoptical model of surveillance.) Unwatched teachers are less likely to comply with the regulations they deem unnecessary or damaging. As a result, 'fabrication' is a frequent response to inspection.[92] Ball takes the term 'fabrication' from Foucault's description of institutional fabrications as accounts of organisations 'that are not altogether true—produced purposefully to be accountable'.[93] These 'staged' or 'choreographed' performances include practiced OfSTED lessons, made-up assessment and work marked in arrears, all worryingly common responses to inspection.[94] It could also be argued that this fabrication contributes to teachers' compliance with OfSTED despite their resistance in principle. Thus, perversely, inspection's pursuit of transparency and accountability has prompted not only distrust but also the generation of quasi and actual deceit.[95] A trust-fostering mechanism is leading teachers into dishonesty. Consequently, not only is the value of inspection under question, yet again it is highlighted that the inspection process in which we have invested so much trust is actually highly untrustworthy.

Thus, whilst audit and accountability processes theoretically protect against risk, they also pose dangers in themselves. In the case of education, this has resulted in schools becoming helplessly caught up in the politics of government education policy—resulting in distortions in practice and outcomes.

6
Conclusion

'Education, education, education', Blair (in)famously declared as his top three priorities whilst in power. During New Labour's nine-year term (at the time of writing) education has irrefutably been at the forefront of the government's political agenda; as a result politics has come to the forefront of school life. Since Blair took power he has made a definitive impact on the country's education, not simply on state schools but on all areas of learning across both sectors. His approach began by exposing the failures of the education system, then by taking control of schools in order to rectify failures. The compelling force of OfSTED was crucial in this improvement-by-commandeering drive. With much greater centrally determined regulation on how schools must teach and assess, OfSTED's role became more than ever one of ensuring adherence to government policy. The strictness of dictation led to a doubling of the number of schools called into 'special measures' by OfSTED in Blair's first term.

Government interference in the independent sector has come as part of New Labour's second wind of educational policing. In an attempt to salvage the legitimacy of state school reforms, there has been an attack on private practice. Rather than tackling its state sector problems, the government has attempted to mitigate them by effectively 'planting' problems in the private sector. By imposing requirements on independent schools, the government has been able to make its schools look better and private schools look worse. Implementing this strategy through an 'independent' inspectorate has prevented it from appearing quite so crude and unjust. Although known to be draconian, OfSTED is not associated with any specific agenda; moreover notions of child protection and health and safety procedure justify the imposition of government regulation. The effect, however, has been to distort the independent market and impose on private schools many of those very policies responsible for the failures of the state sector. Thus, just as in the state system, the flawed nature of imposed policy is generating a discourse of fabrication amongst private schools. Not only are their liberties being sabotaged, they are becoming embroiled in the sabotaging process themselves.

Nevertheless, OfSTED has succeeded in lodging the government's definitions of quality, despite their stark flaws, into the public consciousness. Schools and parents have simply not been able to resist the force of the DfES-cum-OfSTED. This is manifest when previously contented parents withdraw their children from popular private schools with good results but an unsatisfactory OfSTED report; or when head teachers on the orders of OfSTED fork out for educational materials which they deem unnecessary; or when teachers stay up at night fabricating a term of 'invaluable' assessment records.

Had the approaches being forced upon private schools at least proven successful in the state sector, the pill of illegitimate control would be slightly more palatable. We know very well that a significant contributor to the independent sector's continual outstripping of the state in government tests specifically designed to measure the successes of the DfES's strategies is the fact that private schools *don't* do what state schools have to. Rather than taking heed of what the private sector is doing right, the Blair government has concentrated on trying either to exterminate it or demonise it as elitist.

The superior performance of the private sector has been regularly attributed to the 'unfair' advantages accrued by selective intake by academic ability and socio-economic background. Yet more than half of private primary schools are academically non-selective and too much emphasis is placed on the relationship between achievement and background. There is no question that 'good' intake, where pupils come from well-motivated, resourced and supported homes, has a significant impact on learning. This is also manifest within the state sector from disparities in achievement between differing catchment areas. However, it is also evident that middle-class dominated state schools do not do as well as private schools. This is not to do with socio-economic class, but conditions in the classroom.

For the last nine years the single most common reason for parents to move their children from the state to the private sector has been class size.[1] Although the government pronounced that it was trying to entice the middle classes back into the state sector,[2] it has in fact been pushing them into the private. Four years after New Labour came to power there were more pupils per teacher in primary schools than there were under the Conservatives and the pupil:teacher ratio in secondary schools was at its worst level since the 1970s.[3] More recently, as well as comparing badly with the private sector, where the average class size is 14, the UK primary class average of 26.8 pupils also compares badly with the OECD average of 22.1, despite relatively high spending on education in the UK.[4]

Although Blair refused to address class-size (other than in his initial pledge in 1997 for five- to seven-year-olds, which notably was to keep classes below the very high maximum of 30 pupils),[5] it is something now being addressed by New Labour's leader-in-waiting. In his 2006 budget, the 'Education Budget' as it has been termed, Gordon Brown seemed to present greater hope for the future of education in England. Rather than denying the merits of the private sector, he wants to mirror them. His key proposal is to shrink class size by increasing school funding and therefore the number of teachers. However Brown's ensuing expenditure proposals severely miss the point. With the greater total of £8,000 to be spent per pupil, his plan is to provide state school pupils with the technology and premises of the private sector. Had he glanced through a few of OfSTED's reports on private schools, he would have seen that many of them charge *half* that amount and still do better academically. Similarly he would have noticed that many of these schools are actually criticised for having *poor* technology and premises. The answer is not always money, and it is certainly not in the latest technology. Very often it is precisely the 'old-fashioned' teaching methods that OfSTED criticises which account for private school success. Brown has failed to factor in the advantages of less (though decreasingly so) government control on what to teach and how. Rather than having money thrown at them, schools need to be set free to respond to pupil rather than regulatory requirements. Thus, within his plan to recruit more teachers, Brown needs to bear in mind that workload and 'government initiatives', not money, top the list of reasons for the high exit-rate from teaching;[6] equally that whilst good leadership is integral to a school's success, the National Audit Office has just identified the government's regulatory burden as central to the current shortage of head teachers in the state sector.[7]

Part envious, part punitive, the Blair government has persistently penalised the private sector, commencing with anti-elitist rhetoric and culminating in anti-autonomy regulation. The relationship between the private sector and the state sector has been presented as a zero sum equation: as if the successes of private sector pupils are somehow to the detriment of those in the state. Clearly this is a ludicrous assertion and one that has been resorted to out of political necessity. What is to the detriment of the state education system is nothing to do with the 'privileged' private sector but rather with poor government strategy. The problem with the private sector's successes is not that they affect state education, but that they affect the *political education agenda*. A group of schools with no more in common than the fact that they are fee-charging and not wholly controlled by DfES policy are consistently out-stripping state schools. This is a stake through the heart for Blair, whose hoped-for legacy was to annihilate the relationship between class and achievement by taking 'responsibility' for schools.

Failure to reach his pledged targets and failure to close the gap between private and state schools have been very damaging to the credibility of Blair's investment in education. Damage to Blair's credibility has ultimately led to damage to the private sector. OfSTED has been central to attempts to pick up the political pieces; and highlighting the supposed 'inadequacies' of the private sector has been one of them.

That the education system has been crippled by flawed reforms is something educators are only too aware of. Yet, in spite of their reservations, teachers find themselves complicit in the system, thereby perpetuating it. There is a feeling of helplessness as one and all have become tangled up in the contorted tentacles of government control. Vast systemic change is needed to free schools and pupils. But, in the meantime, the rehabilitation of the inspection system back to one of impartial quality assurance is a crucial—and above all, feasible—step. Shooting the messenger, in this case, should be the target.

Recommendations

A thorough review is required by the Education and Skills Select Committee to address the question of OfSTED's independence from governmental influence and how its remit for inspection is determined. Whilst an 'independent validation' of OfSTED's work has been undertaken by the Institute of Education in 2004,[8] it did not examine the fundamental relationship between government policy and the activities of the inspectorate.

General

It is imperative to the proper functioning of the inspectorate that the connection between the government (via the DfES) and OfSTED be severed. Whilst its independence is theoretically enshrined in legislation, its current status as a government department makes it susceptible to political influence.

The Education and Skills Select Committee is the body responsible for scrutinising OfSTED's work. Yet whilst its twice-yearly review addresses an extensive range of concerns, it tends to focus on OfSTED's implementation of directives; furthermore it is overly satisfied with OfSTED's own accountability mechanisms and own judgements regarding its impact on educational provision. Part of the weakness of the Committee in this respect is that it is made up of politicians (MPs, cross-party), not by those working in education. Not being practising educationalists, the Committee does not have a sufficiently insightful grasp of the issues, both practical and pedagogical, surrounding OfSTED's activities. The Committee is in a good position, however, to scrutinise matters such as OfSTED's budget and staffing—as well as the inspectorate's neutrality. OfSTED's work relating to pedagogy needs to be scrutinised by a committee whose members work in different fields of education: across sectors and age groups. The members of the committee, including the chair, would need to change regularly in order to mitigate the dangers of vested interests.

State sector

Whilst theoretically the 'end of the line' for complaints about state school OfSTED inspection is the parliamentary Ombudsman, procedure does not in fact exist for it to consider maintained schools' complaints.[9] Thus the true 'end of the line' for complaints concerning state school inspection is the Independent Complaints Adjudicator. Either way, however, the fundamental problem is that the complaints system is designed to tackle infringements of the terms within which the inspection has been carried out. The underlying assumption, therefore, is that the framework itself is fair and faultless. What is needed is an ombudsman to monitor the very principles of the OfSTED inspection process.

Serving teachers should become a part of inspection teams, a proposal supported by several key educational institutions such as the General Teaching Council, the Institute of Education and the Learning and Skills Development Agency.[10] This 'peer review' element would be beneficial to schools as the teacher would not be ensconced in the inspection system as well as being more in touch with the realities of school life. (The 'impartial from OfSTED' element was part of the justification for the recently discarded 'lay inspectors'; however, they were not teachers.) It would also help OfSTED to identify genuine implementations from those temporarily employed for inspection purposes. This would help determine the true effectiveness of education policies. It is this type of teacher involvement, as seen in the Independent Schools Inspectorate inspections, which is likely to foster a more constructive relationship between school life and inspection.

The inspection process needs to be longer, not shorter, and less, not more, frequent. This would also facilitate the deployment of teachers in inspection (as recommended above). Unless there is a high teacher turnover, a school should not be able to 'transform' in five years (based on the previous six-year inspection cycle). However, if inspection criteria deal with superficial aspects of a school as they do now, then a transformation over a five-year period is not just possible, but likely. This is a reflection on the shallow manner in which schools are being judged. Schools causing concern, reflected previously in indicators such as high teacher turnover, high pupil truancy and absence, can be monitored instead by the LEA. In its new role as 'guardian of standards' (proposed in the 2006 Education and Inspections Bill), the LEA could usefully take on more of the 'improving' role, particularly in the above areas, removing this potentially contentious duty from OfSTED.

Private sector

Private schools should not be expected to fulfil any DfES regulation on educational provision. Independent schools should not have to comply with regulation concerning teaching content and style but only with regulation concerning issues of basic health and safety and child protection. These issues are currently buried in the minutiae of discussions about the 'quality' of education. Concern that the removal of scrutiny over educational content will not safeguard against harmful teaching (for example that inciting discrimination) can be addressed by non-education related legislation.

Within the complaints process for independent schools lies the potential for making complaints about OfSTED inspection to the parliamentary Ombudsman, as well as to the Independent Complaints Adjudicator. However, the rigidity of the complaints procedure and what is judged to be a legitimate complaint—when the terms of the inspection framework have been violated—means that although extensive procedure *exists* it is not necessarily available in practice. In the document 'Complaints about independent school inspections' OfSTED makes clear that there is no guarantee that complaints presented to the Independent Complaints Adjudicator and the Ombudsman will actually be considered.

One possible way to defend their freedoms would be for non-association independent schools to form their own representative body. The establishment of such a body specifically for non-association head teachers would create an affordable and unobtrusive lobbying force.

In order to preserve its autonomy in the current climate, the independent sector needs to start fighting for it. What is ultimately needed is an uprising against the current level of statutory requirement for private schools. Although OfSTED is the enforcer of these straitjacketing directives, protest needs to be directed towards the DfES as the source of the problem. The difficulty is that this would require either co-ordination on the part of non-association schools (which would be hard to achieve) or the clout of a well-established (and for practical purposes, well-off) school, to have an impact. The fact is that the schools best placed to protest against central intervention are the country's top public schools. Yet, as discussed in chapter 4, these schools, which are members of the Independent Schools Council, are for a number of reasons reluctant to take a public stance against the government's requirements. However, while equally not isolating themselves from the rest of the education system, it is important that schools in the ISC re-evaluate their relationship with the government.

Reforming education policy

A major contributor to the malfunctions within the inspection system, though extraneous to its own mechanisms, is the process of education policy formation. Education reforms over the last nine years have raised serious issues over the very basis of the policy-making process. Under the New Labour government in particular (but also in previous administrations) inadequately trialled school initiatives have been implemented nation-wide. Indeed, one of the greatest flaws in this government's school improvement drive has been the continual turnover of its reforms and the rapidity with which they have been applied.

A safeguard is required to prevent governments from being able to pass legislation without sufficient evidence that it will be effective in schools. Slowing down the reformation process may sound dangerous, yet the adverse effects of constant change, particularly when continuity is so vital in schooling, are far greater than slowing down the implementation of potentially beneficial policy.

Finally, and this point cannot be stressed enough, for progress and excellence to be fostered, it is imperative that central control over pedagogy, curriculum and outcome is loosened. This does not mean leaving schools to do simply as they please and it does not mean shutting the door on accountability. It means giving teachers the flexibility to respond to their pupils and judging the success of their strategies on genuine learning outcomes—well-functioning accountability—rather than the effectiveness of their test preparation. Under New Labour the primary sector has been beleaguered with paperwork and calls to teach to the test, resulting from the lethal combination of over-regulation and pressure to reach government targets. In 1997, responding to the new government's proposals for tight central planning, Lord Skidelsky argued that it would lead to highly problematic rigidity. His predictions could not have been more accurate:

> ... you can't easily undo something that turns out to be unsuccessful when it has the force of the law behind it. Nor does it increase accountability since statistics can always be given the spin that is wanted. Moreover, as things don't go well, the controllers get anxious, and the 'ubiquity of cheating' is stepped up.[11]

Appendix 1
Charterhouse Square School: 2004

The Charterhouse Square School, founded in 1985 by the present head teacher, Mrs Jamie Malden, is an independent day school for boys and girls aged from three to eleven. The school occupies a five-storey Victorian building overlooking Charterhouse Square in the City of London. There are 171 pupils on the roll and the annual school fees are £7,650. The school's ethos is based on the belief that a happy and stimulating environment is an essential basis for high standards of academic achievement. It aims to:

- recognise and provide for the fact that each child is an individual;
- plan a curriculum of individual as well as shared experiences;
- develop a good work ethic, a good attention span, an ability to work independently and to follow group instructions.[1]

Preparation of pupils for admission to independent schools of their choice is also a principal priority. The school feeds a large number of pupils into top secondary schools such as the City of London schools and Westminster. Whilst the SATs are not statutory for independent schools, Charterhouse Square School has opted to participate in them—with outstanding results. Over the years the school has successfully maintained a consistent record of SATs results well above the national average.[2]

In March 2004 Charterhouse Square was inspected by OfSTED. Following a three-day inspection, OfSTED reported very unfavourably on the education provided by Charterhouse Square School. The school was ordered by the inspectorate to rectify identified weaknesses by drawing up and implementing an 'action plan'.[3] Failure to make the advised amendments could lead to the school's closure.[4]

The OfSTED report

Charterhouse Square School was charged around £6,000 for the inspection, calculated on the basis of the number of pupils in the school. Two inspectors conducted the inspection, one responsible for reporting on the quality of the school's infant section, the other for the junior section.

On top of their academic record, Charterhouse Square School's pupils were described by OfSTED as 'happy, secure and self-confident' with 'well-developed literacy, oracy and numeracy skills'.[5] Nevertheless, the following weaknesses were identified in the school's educational provision:

- narrowly defined curriculum;[6]
- over-emphasis on English and maths;[7]
- insufficient documentation of plans and schemes of work;[8]
- insufficient implementation of lesson plans;[9]
- insufficient design and technology;[10]
- insufficient ICT;[11]
- inappropriate Early Years curriculum;[12]
- over-reliance on prescriptive workbooks;[13]
- over-emphasis on preparation for secondary school entrance exams;[14]
- lack of cross-curricula links;[15]
- insufficient differentiation of work according to pupil ability;[16]
- learning objectives are not made clear to the pupils;[17]
- there are few opportunities for pupils to work collaboratively;[18]

- inadequate assessment;[19]
- inadequate detail in marking;[20]
- resources do not support the development of individual investigative learning skills;[21]
- too few opportunities for educational visits.[22]

Teaching was regarded as 'instructional', lacking inspiration, with tasks 'often dull and repetitive': the implication was that the educational provision was old-fashioned, with undue focus on the 3 Rs, thus presenting 'little opportunity for pupil creativity'.[23] The school also failed to meet the following criteria relating to other areas:

- compliance with 'the welfare, health and safety of the pupils' requirements: on the grounds that there is no written health and safety policy for school educational visits;[24]
- compliance with the 'the suitability of the proprietor and staff' requirements: on the grounds that not all staff have been cleared by the CRB;[25]
- compliance with the 'the suitability of the premises and accommodation' requirements: *on the grounds that the integrated chairs and tables are too large and inappropriate for pupils.*[26]

Appendix 2
Two Case Studies

OfSTED intervention is both thwarting the successes and autonomy of good private schools and exacerbating the difficulties faced by struggling schools in the state sector. Two case studies have been taken to illustrate the adverse effects which OfSTED inspections can have. The nature of the information provided by the schools about their inspection has made it necessary to disguise them.

The first school is a successful prep school in Cambridge; the second, a struggling primary school in a deprived London borough. The schools were followed over the course of two years, following their inspection and the aftermath. Both schools received poor inspection reports and were required to make considerable alterations to their provision within specified periods. The private school failed four out of the seven sets of regulations, and the state school was identified as having 'serious weaknesses'. In the private school case study, improvement required significant changes, from teaching and assessment practice to physical environment. In the state school case study, improvement involved higher attainment and more stringent application of government policy. Both schools took drastic measures to meet the required changes. The private school has since been re-inspected successfully, with OfSTED very satisfied with their 'improvement'; the state school has been judged to be on course in its improvement programme. The outcomes for the schools have, however, been less satisfactory. The private school has had to spend large sums on measures that at best they believe to be not helpful to learning, at worst to be actually detrimental, as well as losing popularity as a result of its adverse report. The state school has witnessed an extremely high staff turnover because of the pressures of the inspection process as well as facing continuous distraction from actual teaching and learning.

The private case: Melbury House

In early 2004 Melbury House in Cambridge was a very successful non-selective prep school. Charging approximately £8,000 a year, the school had a full roll of around 200 pupils and a waiting list. Catering for children between three and eleven, the school consistently achieved high SATs results, had brought many children up to two years beyond their reading age and held an excellent record of feeding its pupils into selective secondary schools of their choice. In the twenty years since its foundation, Melbury House had been inspected several times under the old inspection system of Her Majesty's Inspectors (HMIs) with excellent outcomes. Consequently, in order to avoid pre-inspection stress for her teachers, when OfSTED announced its inspection date six weeks in advance, the head teacher and proprietor, Miss Smith, decided to take the inspection in the school's stride. She undertook no additional preparation for the inspection, made no changes to daily routine, and informed her staff about the inspection only three days before. Miss Smith mentioned that the Lead Inspector had asked her what preparations she had undertaken for the inspection. Miss Smith described the inspector as 'visibly shocked' to hear that the answer was 'none'. (This is despite the fact that officially OfSTED specifically advises schools to not undertake any preparation for inspection.) As the deputy head, Mrs Walker commented:

> OfSTED inspection is a very artificial process: we didn't prepare for inspection and instead opened our doors with total honesty—but rather than this being commendable, we were penalised for it.

OfSTED found that Melbury House failed to fulfil four out of the seven necessary regulatory categories, performing particularly badly in the category relating to teaching and learning. Despite the school's strong academic record, Melbury House stumbled on every possible count to do with the 'quality of the education provided by the school'. The school's curriculum and documentation were inadequate, as were its teaching, assessment procedures and its resources.

Following the inspection, Melbury House was required to draw up an Action Plan outlining how it planned to address the weaknesses identified by OfSTED. The Action Plan was to be submitted to OfSTED for approval within 28 days. Once it had been approved, Melbury House implemented the proposed 'action', to be inspected in a follow-up inspection. The school addressed each of the above criticisms, making all the changes necessary to fulfil the DfES's regulations. Miss Smith described the curriculum as resultantly 'revolutionised' with the implementation of the National Curriculum followed 'to the t'. She noted that in doing so the school discovered that in several cases their pupils were over two years ahead of the government's guidelines:

> In Year 6 literacy [following the government's guidelines], for example, pupils are learning about verbs—something our children have covered more than two years earlier!

The demands for paperwork were met in full; new plans and schemes of work were written out and implemented, new teaching strategies introduced and all the school's policy documents re-written. Extensive material changes were also made, such as the building of a computer suite, and numerous new teaching resources were purchased.

OfSTED's three days in Melbury House transformed life for the school. The inspection imposed great costs on the school both financially and in terms of popularity. Although no parents removed their pupils after the inspection, the following year eight prospective parents withdrew their children's registrations. One of these parents even sued the school for 'false description'. This parent felt he was entitled to reclaim his non-refundable deposit because of the school's unexpectedly negative OfSTED report. Miss Smith however refused to reimburse the parent. Her argument was that the parent had chosen Melbury House on the basis of the prospectus which, regardless of the OfSTED judgement, continued to be a valid guide to the school's provision. Miss Smith won the case on these grounds.

Two years on, for the first time in 20 years, instead of a waiting list there are 20 vacancies. Since the inspection Miss Smith has had to work much harder to sell the school to prospective parents. Miss Smith has calculated that in its entirety the inspection experience has cost Melbury House a crippling total of £198,000. This is in expenses both directly connected to the inspection, for example the charge of the inspection itself, and in costs relating to the repercussions. These 'repercussions' entailed expenditure on measures to meet OfSTED's requirements such as new furniture, enlarging a classroom and additional computers, as well as measures to salvage the school from the damage of a poor OfSTED report. These included paying £30 a month for a website company to ensure that internet searches bring up the school's website before OfSTED's inspection report; hiring a deputy head 'well-versed' in the inspection process; and paying £800 a day for the services of a commercial inspection consultant.

The school's response to OfSTED's inspection

Interestingly both Miss Smith, the head, and Mrs Walker, the deputy head, thought that there was an 'unquestionable need' for *state* regulation of the independent sector: however, the level of prescription was vitally important. Miss Smith felt very strongly that this should not mean removing individual initiative and personal style, elements which she considered to be rendering the current system fundamentally flawed. She saw educational choice as the prerogative of the consumer, emphasising that parents should be able to decide for themselves how they spend their money. Moreover, she argued that the current style of inspection was unnecessary for private schools as the reality was that by charging fees independent schools were significantly *more* accountable than state schools.

Miss Smith regarded the current government's attitude to education as 'bullying'. Schools were being homogenised in the state sector and through government diktat the same was now happening in the private sector. But as Mrs Walker pointed out: 'independent schools' very *raison d'être* is doing things differently—what's the point in being independent otherwise?' Both teachers felt that in this sense the former HMI system of inspection had been hugely superior, as 'HMI used to *value* these differences in independent schools' (Mrs Walker, deputy head).

'How independent *is* independent?' was Miss Smith's complaint about the government's intervention into the private education sector. Rather than testing the quality of education, she considered inspection to be more about testing preparation for inspection: 'Why else would they give you six weeks to prepare in?'

Pedagogically, Miss Smith considered the state system to be overly child-centred, enforcing innovation in pedagogy where it was not desirable. She also felt that the huge importance given to documenting teacher action and logs on each child's learning was 'superfluous paper pushing', invariably involving teachers forfeiting actual teaching time. Miss Smith was keen to point out that the majority of Melbury House's teachers had left the state sector through disillusionment with the quantity of pointless paperwork and teaching conditions more generally.

> ***Freedom of choice is being squeezed out of schools, as the government becomes increasingly narrow-minded: the state education system is starting to remind me of Russian communist education where every child is on the same page on any given day.***
>
> *Miss Smith, head teacher Melbury House*

Miss Smith was frustrated by the fact that although all the private school head teachers whom she knew disagreed with OfSTED's inspection of the private sector, they were not prepared to 'rise up'. Whilst she considered other heads to be overly willing to comply, she recognised from her own experience how 'too much was at stake'.

Independent schools feel very vulnerable to OfSTED's power—and criticising OfSTED puts schools in danger of OfSTED criticising *them*. Miss Smith highlighted the problematic nature of independent schools' relationship with OfSTED:

> Some of it's not even statutory regulation but 'recommendation'. For example, the lead inspector recommended that we stopped marking in red pen and stopped using crosses. Now I disagree quite strongly with this, but you find yourself in the position where it's very difficult to resist [these suggestions].

The combination of this type of 'voluntary' compliance with unwritten and non-statutory policy makes it even more problematic for schools to defend their independence. This difficulty of disagreeing with OfSTED relates to the 'rigid checklist' focus and lack of dialogue in inspection. Miss Smith illustrated this with her attempted defence against OfSTED's criticism that Melbury House lacked resources. When Miss Smith tried to show the inspector 'the cupboards full of resources', the inspector refused to take them into account on the grounds that there was no *documented* evidence for them.

The re-inspection

Two weeks prior to the follow-up inspection Melbury House received an email from OfSTED informing them of the date that the inspectors would be coming to the school. (Miss Smith was thus very surprised to later hear that schools are not supposed to be given more than a term-long time frame and then only 48 hours notice of a follow-up inspection.)

The two inspectors in OfSTED's second inspection were 'very pleased' with the changes the school had made, particularly in its educational provision. To the school's 'amazement' (Mrs Walker), the inspectors told the school that it would not be inspected again for another six years. Why Melbury House found this so surprising was because the follow-up inspection had looked solely at the regulations which the school had failed in the last inspection. Miss Smith and Mrs Walker had since identified that the school still did not fulfil several other major regulatory requirements. These were mainly health and safety related regulations: for example, classroom doors opened inwardly instead of outwardly, something which is against the regulatory requirements for fire safety; pupil washbasins did not have running hot water, the issue which OfSTED had battled so forcefully over with South School; and pupil toilets were not single-sex—an issue OfSTED had also forcefully battled over in Summerhill's inspection. Melbury House was also aware that its current marking policy did not fulfil OfSTED's requirements. However, in this instance the inspectors had a particular set of boxes to tick and that was their only remit, regardless of the fact that this approach defied OfSTED's overall remit of ensuring compliance with all the DfES's regulatory requirements.

Thus, Melbury House is finally in the clear. A positive re-inspection report in the public domain will help to counteract the damage done by OfSTED and allow the school to rebuild its reputation. But will Melbury House continue to implement all the pedagogic concessions it had made for OfSTED? 'No, we cannot afford to—a drop, just one year, in our academic performance would be very damaging', was Miss Smith's response.

The state case: St George's

St George's is a small primary school in a London borough. St George's is a Church of England school, although the vast majority of its pupils are Muslim. The borough is one of the most deprived in the country and the number of unemployed is roughly three times the national average. Consequently St George's has an above average number of children entitled to school meals (a commonly used poverty indicator). Apart from pupil poverty, St George's also faces other difficulties. With around 99 per cent of the pupils having English as their second language, getting them to communicate with each other in English is difficult. As a result even pupils who have been at the school since Reception speak and write comparatively poor English. The majority of these children's parents speak either poor English or none at all, meaning that they are unable to help their children with schoolwork. This issue is exacerbated by the fact that pupils are frequently taken out of school for extended visits to their countries of origin, leaving gaps in both their education and their progress in English. Teacher turnover has also been enormously disruptive to pupils' learning, with some classes having had a series of very short-term supply teachers. In a vicious cycle, low standards in the school, low test results and high absence rates mean that the school has been targeted by government education authorities, whose intervention has led to teachers leaving and to the school having to prioritise central targets rather than their pupils' learning (the two, all too often, not being synonymous).

In 2004, within the then six-year inspection cycle system, St George's was due for an inspection. St George's 'vital statistics' made it a prime target for local education authority (LEA) intervention. It had a record of low SATs results at both Key Stage 1 and 2, both in absolute and value-added terms (attainment measured by progress), no permanent head teacher, very high teacher-turnover and under-subscribed classes. The LEA consequently subjected the school to what might be described as a course of 'shock therapy' in preparation for inspection. School life was turned upside down as an army of LEA consultants stepped in whose job it was to bolster pupil performance levels, and to ensure that teachers were carrying out the DfES's teaching directives and producing the prerequisite 'paperwork' to prove it.

The work of the LEA in schools like St George's demonstrates the lengths which LEAs go to in order to prepare schools for inspection. In 2004 the primary role of the LEA in deprived areas was to bring up the 'standard' of its schools. Although the 2005 Education and Inspection Bill has altered the role of the LEA, its newly defined remit of 'champion of standards' will mean little alteration to its activities in poorer parts of the country. Similarly, although OfSTED has adopted a different inspection schedule, their treatment of struggling schools remains largely unchanged.

The LEA School Improvement Team

As a low-performing local authority, school improvement is a key priority for the borough. A group of LEA officers form what can be termed the school improvement team (SIT). The team relevant to the primary sector consists of a five-tiered hierarchy made up of the director of education and social services, the head of school improvement, the head of primary strategy, five school development advisers, three literacy consultants and three numeracy consultants.

'Zero tolerance', whereby low test performance on the grounds of socio-economic deprivation is not accepted, lay at the heart of the SIT's existence. The SIT's overall mission was to bring all schools' test performance up to the national average and to have no schools receiving poor inspection reports from OfSTED. In July 2004 a number of the SIT were interviewed on their role in the process of preparing low-performing schools for inspection.

There is, unsurprisingly, a large attainment and inspection gap between deprived areas and the national average; the SIT's main focus was to close this gap as rapidly as possible. Terms such as 'benchmark', 'standard', 'floor target', 'level', and 'threshold' littered the SIT's responses. Measures of achievement and progress were captured by nationally determined definitions and levels, thus allowing success to only be measured in standardised and thereby comparable terms.

The way in which the members of the SIT championed this drive bordered on evangelical, with much sloganeering in the interviews. Yet the occasional critical disclosure undermined the value of the entire improvement strategy. Criticism was, however, fearfully reluctant, with *'I shouldn't be saying this'* becoming a common refrain. One of the school development advisers (SDA) identified an inherent problem in preparing schools for inspection as the fact that schools were 'patched together' using short-term strategies. She cited an example of a school identified by the SIT as having 'critical weaknesses' which six weeks later received a 'very good' OfSTED judgement:

> The problem is that often the changes are unsustainable, ones that will get the school through OfSTED, but do not make a good school when it's all over.

The SIT's philosophy was 'input is inverse to achievement' (SDA). Therefore 'if a school is weak, it will be inundated [by the LEA] in the run-up to OfSTED' (SDA). Statistics on schools' achievement and comparative achievement were central to the SIT's operations, and the borough even had a 'Statistics and Research Team'.

The general consensus amongst the SIT was that schools were unable to improve on their own. Schools were thought to need 'motivational forces... because left to themselves the schools don't follow things through often', (literacy consultant). As one interviewee commented, the SIT was in a good position to implement change and improvement, as they were able to be 'more critical, more detached' (SDA). A school's senior management team, on the other hand, was constrained by 'that need for diplomacy'(SDA).

St George's preparation for inspection

At the start of the 2004 academic year a 'super head' was brought in to St George's to spend a term working closely with the SIT ensuring the implementation of the most imperative changes in preparation for OfSTED. For the remainder of the year the deputy head teacher became acting head. As OfSTED did not inspect the school until the first term of the next academic year, the school was subjected to LEA intervention for an entire year. Between September 2003 and September 2004 there was a record teacher turnover; as well as the change to the headship, the Nursery class had two different teachers, Year 2 had three, Year 4 had two and Year 5 had three.

Over the year the SIT carried out 30 whole-school teaching observations. For the teachers, each lesson observation meant making extra teaching resources, additional and more detailed planning, and in some instances actually practising the lesson. As well as finding the preparation for lesson observations very stressful, the teachers interviewed found the generally critical feedback very demoralising:

> There are lots of issues to tackle teaching in a school like this, but it's the [SIT's] criticisms thrown at your teaching constantly that get you down.
>
> Year 2 teacher

> It makes me angry that my dedication to the children is being undermined: they [the SIT] make you feel guilty—you have never done enough.
>
> Year 4 teacher

Together with the pressure of constant scrutiny, the castigatory approach to 'improvement' taken by the LEA was a key reason for the school's high staff turnover:

> Being told you are not doing it right all the time, despite the hours and effort you put in, just makes you think eventually 'I've had enough of this' and leave. Teachers, good teachers, leaving all the time isn't making the school any better.
>
> Year 3 teacher

A main aim of the SIT in St George's was to ensure that DfES teaching directives were being implemented. One of the greatest areas of contention from the interviewed teachers were the u-turns in these directives:

> In the first term we were 'floating facilitators'; the next term they [the DFES] had changed their mind, now we were only supposed to work with a small group; and by the final term it was whole class teaching—mustn't work with small groups!
>
> Year 5 teacher

Three different teachers mentioned the summer term's new teaching buzzword, 'interactive teaching', which had involved reorganising their teaching structure. 'It's very fickle', commented the Year 1 class teacher, 'their [the DfES's] teaching policies are short-lived—seasonal change.'

The Year 5 teacher illustrated the ever-changing nature of policy with her class's literacy exercise books. Central directives enforced by the SIT had instructed pupils to write the 'learning intention' in three different ways intermittently through the year: 'My class joke about the changes now', she laughed, 'they come in on a Monday and say "Miss, how should we do the Learning Intention this week?"'

SATs results were of great importance to the SIT, as they affected both the borough's league table performance and OfSTED's judgement of a school. The teachers for Year 2 and Year 6, the years in which there is statutory testing, were sent on numerous SATs-related courses at the LEA's Professional Development Centre. Amongst other things, these courses gave teachers advice and 'tips': tips which included teaching only the tested subjects (numeracy and literacy in Year 2, and also science in Year 6). The SIT advised the school to hold 'booster' classes for pupils taking the tests, and to focus on the middle level achievers whilst more or less ignoring the top and bottom of the class in order to reach attainment targets.

All the interviewed teachers resented the LEA's strategies but they conceded that although they 'moaned amongst themselves', they complied without resistance—or left. The deputy head described the LEA's relationship with the school as a 'dictatorship'. She felt that there had been a 'real climate change', with the LEA having taken on 'an inspector guise instead of being advisory'. She attributed this to the current emphasis on OfSTED performance. The Year 6 teacher also reflected on how there used to 'more of a dialogue' between schools and the LEA. She too attributed the change to the high profile of inspection outcomes.

At the beginning of the autumn term, 'the brown envelope' finally arrived: St George's was to be inspected in six weeks. Would the LEA's intervention pay off? 'SATs results have risen slightly but still don't meet the targets', commented the Year 1 teacher, 'and six members of staff are leaving this year—so all the work done with them won't be seen by OfSTED anyway.' Ironically, staff departure, largely attributable to the SIT's activities, would counteract the SIT's impact on OfSTED's inspection judgement.

> ***St George's has lost a lot of staff throughout the year... the LEA has definitely influenced those resignations.***
>
> *Reception teacher*

The inspection

Four new teachers had been hired for the autumn term, and a new head started a couple of weeks before the inspection. In their interviews at the end of the previous school year, the school had deliberately not mentioned that St George's was expecting an inspection. From a teaching perspective the school was already fairly undesirable; knowledge of an imminent inspection would have acted as a further deterrent.

During the six weeks prior to the inspection, the LEA 'went overboard' in the school (Reception—former Year 1—teacher). At this stage the main focus was ensuring that teachers' had the prerequisite 'written evidence'. Lesson planning files had to be meticulously in order, and backdated plans redone if they did not contain sufficient detail; the SIT went through checklists of paperwork demands which the school needed quickly to create in order to demonstrate that they had been in full function. Teachers were even instructed to go through their marking of pupils' old work and fill out comments where comments were not elaborate enough.

By the week of the inspection the school had undergone a temporary transformation—or, in the words of the Reception teacher, 'a big fat show'.

In the last few days before the inspection, members of the SIT had come in to put up displays—allegedly done by the teachers. In the Nursery class, where the teacher had not co-operated in inspection preparations, the SIT themselves had done up the classroom and even 'planted' artificial past plans into the Nursery teacher's planning folder: 'The Nursery class was completely fixed and fake for the inspection', complained the Reception teacher.

OfSTED's judgement was that the school had 'serious weaknesses', just one step up from 'special measures', the most serious category; this meant that OfSTED would monitor St George's progress until the school was re-inspected after roughly two years. The Year 5 teacher felt that the school had been unfairly put into the 'serious weaknesses' category: 'The inspectors said that they didn't think the school could improve fast enough—so they put it in 'serious weaknesses'. But, as she pointed out, 'the [new] head teacher had been in the school for only a couple of weeks before the inspection', and four new members of staff had started just the month earlier. What had ultimately been responsible for OfSTED's damning judgement was the school's Key Stage 2 SATs results. Considering the recentness of so many of the staff's appointments and the fact that only two observed lessons had been graded 'unsatisfactory', the Year 5 teacher thought that the inspectorate's criticism of the school's SATs results was unwarranted. Another defence of the SATs results was the instability of the school's intake. A significant number of Year 6 pupils had not spent much time in the school, and others had spent extended time away from school in their countries of origin. However, 'the inspectors said they couldn't take any excuses' (Year 5 teacher).

Had OfSTED's inspection helped the school? 'No, it was totally destructive', was the Year 5 teacher's response. 'Not only did it not improve anything, it actually *slowed down* the improvement process—it took us two months to recover from the inspection.'

After the inspection, two class teachers—including the Nursery teacher—left St George's. Although the SIT has 'disappeared' since the inspection—'apart from to take back their stuff' (Reception teacher)—OfSTED continues to be very much on the school's mind. School life still revolves heavily around inspection priorities; there is a constant stream of documentation generation such as assessment, tracking and planning, as well as continual meetings about these activities. 'It's all about evidence, evidence that we are raising achievement' (Year 5 teacher). Key Stage 2 SATs performance is also central to the improvement process with a series of 'booster' strategies implemented to drive up this year's Key Stage 2 SATs scores: 'The new head teacher is great', observed the Reception teacher, 'preparation for inspection is now happening all year—we have everything in place and can now produce any document at any time.' And has this furthered learning in the school? 'Oh no! It's all rubbish, all this is for OfSTED, it doesn't help teaching at all.' According to David Bell, former Chief Inspector:

> The designation of a school as... having 'serious weaknesses' may be challenging for head teachers, teachers and governors, but I make no apology for this. The children and young people who are getting a raw deal deserve better.[1]

However, when research[2] confirms the obvious—that good teachers are imperative to schools with a disadvantaged intake—it is difficult to see how the damaging intervention of the inspection process is itself not a 'raw deal'.

Notes

Introduction

1. OfSTED, *How We Inspect Independent Schools,* 'What are the results of an independent school inspection?' (http://www.ofsted.gov.uk/howwework/index.cfm?fuseaction =howwework.inspections&id=5)
2. Independent Schools Council, *Facts and Figures,* 'Numbers'. (http://www.isc.co.uk/index.php/5).
3. OfSTED inspector in interview, 24 January 2006.
4. Statutory Instruments: 2003 No. 1910: Education, England, 'The Education (Independent School Standards) (England) Regulations 2003 as amended 17 January 2005'.
5. Independent Schools Council, *2005-2006 Snapshot: Independent Schooling in the United Kingdom*, 2005.
6. BBC Online, 'Blair's Legacy for Schools', 19 May 2006.
7. Department for Education and Skills, Foreword by the Prime Minister, *White Paper: Higher Standards, Better Schools for All: More Choice for Parents and Pupils'*, October 2005.
8. 'Shortage of teachers as schools debt soars to £120m', *Daily Telegraph,* 29 January 2006.
9. Note: the assisted places scheme, established in 1980 (under the premiership of Margaret Thatcher) in which the government subsidised private school fees, was abolished in 1997 (under the premiership of Tony Blair).
10. Bell, R., European Forum for Freedom in Education, *Country report: United Kingdom, in Atlas of Human Rights to Education and Freedom of Schooling in Europe*, Borchert, M. and Bell, R. (eds), EFFE, Bochum, 2004. (www.effe-eu.org/).
11. Interview with Chris Woodhead, 3 February 2006.
12. Unnamed members of the Education and Skills Select Committee.
13. Mansell, W., *Times Education Supplement,* 1 March 2003 quoted in Smithers, A., 'Education policy', in Seldon, A. (ed.), *The Blair Effect,* London: Little Brown, 2001.

14 Smithers, 'Education policy', in *The Blair Effect*, 2001, p. 2.

15 Department for Education and Skills, The Standards Site Forum, 'Estelle Morris speaks out', 9 January 2003.

16 Adonis A., Let Blair be his own education chief', *Observer*, 15 December 1996.

17 Wikipedia: Ted Wragg (http://en.wikipedia.org/wiki/Ted_Wragg).

18 Adonis, 'Let Blair be his own education chief', *Observer*, 15 December 1996.

19 Smithers, 'Education policy', in *The Blair Effect*, 2001.

20 Hill, D., 'The Third Way in Britain: New Labour's neo-liberal education policy', paper presented at Congres Marx International III, Universite de Paris-X Nanterre-Sorbonne, September 2001. Note: In 1998 and 1999, expenditure on education was 4.55 of GDP, a lower level than under Thatcher, when it fell to 4.7 per cent of GDP.

21 'MP's to give OfSTED a "going-over"', *Guardian*, 14 October 2003.

22 Docking, J., 'Curriculum Initiatives' in Docking, J. (ed.), *New Labour's Policies in Schools: Raising the Standard?*, London: David Fulton Publishers, 2000.

23 Department for Education and Skills, National Curriculum Assessments of 11 year olds in England, 2005, (Provisional). (http://www.dfes.gov.uk/ rsgateway/DB/SFR/s000611/SFR47-2005v1.pdf). Note: only 57 per cent of pupils in 2005 achieved level 4 in both the reading and writing components of the English test and the Maths test.

24 House of Commons Education and Skills Committee, *Teaching Children to Read, Eighth Report of Session 2004-05*, 21 March 2005.

25 Curriculum, Evaluation and Management Centre (CEM), Durham University: Performance Indicators in Primary Schools (PIPS) Project: Standards Over Time 2002. (www.pipsproject.org/standardsovertime.asp).

26 'Children are less able than they used to be', *Guardian*, 24 January 2006.

27 Smithers, 'Education policy', in *The Blair Effect*, 2001, p. 9.

1: OfSTED the Enforcer

1. Smithers, A., 'Education policy', in Seldon, A. (ed.), *The Blair Effect*, London: Little Brown, 2001.
2. '"Cowed" teachers rely on tests not assessment', *Times Educational Supplement*, 22 July 2004.
3. House of Commons, Select Committee on Education and Employment, Fourth Report, 'The work of OfSTED: report from the education sub-committee: the history of HMI and the establishment of OfSTED', 1999. (http://www.publications.parliament.uk/pa/cm199899/cmselect/cmeduemp/62/6205.htm#a3).
4. Coffey, A., *Education and Social Change*, Buckingham: Open University Press, 2001.
5. Chitty, C. and Dunford, J., 'Introduction' in *State Schools: New Labour and the Conservative Legacy*, London: Woburn Press, 1999, p. 3.
6. Chitty and Dunford, 'Introduction,' in *State Schools*, 1999, p. 3.
7. Chitty and Dunford, 'Introduction,' in *State Schools*, 1999, p. 3.
8. OfSTED, 'One-stop shop inspection service', *OfSTED Direct*, Issue 5, Spring Term 05/06.
9. House of Commons, 'Minutes of evidence taken before the Education and Skills Select Committee: the work of OfSTED: uncorrected transcript', November 2005.
10. Power, M., *The Audit Explosion*, London: Demos, 1994.
11. Ferguson, N., Earley, P., Fidler, B. and Ouston, J., *Improving Schools and Inspection: the Self-inspecting School*, London: Chapman, 2000.
12. David Bell, OfSTED Annual Report 2004/2005.
13. Webb. R. *et al.*, 1998, quoted in Coffey, *Education and Social Change*, 2001, p. 14.
14. Webb. R. *et al.*, quoting head a teacher, 1998, cited in Coffey, *Education and Social Change*, 2001, p. 14.
15. Shaw, D., 'Target Setting, Inspection and Assessment' in Docking, J. (ed.), *New Labour's Policies for Schools: Raising the Standard?*, London: David Fulton Publishers, 2000.

16 BBC News Online, 'Schools, fail a million pupils', 11 January 2006.

17 BBC News Online, 'OfSTED tells on teachers', 20 January 2006.

18 'My school's the best because I ignored Labour', *Daily Mail*, 2 December 2005.

19 National Union of Teachers, *The Response of the NUT to the OfSTED Consultation: The Future of Inspection*, 2004. (http://www.teachers.org.uk/resources/word/NUT_Rspns-Futue_of_Inspection.doc).

20 House of Commons, 'Minutes of evidence taken before the Education and Skills Select Committee: the work of OfSTED: uncorrected transcript', November 2005.

21 OfSTED, *About us*. (http://www.ofsted.gov.uk/howwework/).

22 OfSTED, *Inspection of Non-association Independent Schools*, July 2005.

23 Interview with OfSTED inspector, 24 January 2006.

24 OfSTED, *About us*. (http://www.ofsted.gov.uk/howwework/).

25 OfSTED, *About us*. (http://www.ofsted.gov.uk/howwework/).

26 Interview with Chris Woodhead, 3 February 2006.

27 OfSTED, *Departmental Report 2005-06*, 'About OfSTED', May 2006.

28 House of Commons, 'Minutes of evidence taken before the Education and Skills Select Committee: the work of OfSTED: uncorrected transcript', November 2005.

29 'OfSTED condemns foundation-stage profiling', *Times Educational Supplement*, 21 May 2004.

30 'OfSTED slates skills of staff', *Times Education Supplement*, 12 December 2003.

31 'OfSTED chief worried at plans for assistants to cover for teachers', *Guardian*, 17 September 2002.

32 Anonymous Labour member of the Education and Skills Select Committee, in interview, January 2006.

33 Interview with Chris Woodhead, 3 February 2006.

2: OfSTED in the State Sector

1 OfSTED, Barton Church of England Primary School (inspection report) (http://www.ofsted.gov.uk/reports/110/110829.pdf);

OfSTED, Cheam Fields Primary School (inspection report) (http://www.ofsted.gov.uk/reports/102/102964.pdf);

OfSTED, Fern Hill Primary School (inspection report) (http://www.ofsted.gov.uk/reports/131/131097.pdf);

OfSTED, Burlington Junior School (inspection report) (http://www.ofsted.gov.uk/reports/102/102564.pdf).

2 OfSTED, Barton Church of England Primary School (inspection report), 'Part A: Summary of the report: Overall evaluation'; OfSTED, Cheam Fields Primary School (inspection report), 'Part A: Summary of the report: Overall evaluation'; OfSTED, Fern Hill Primary School (inspection report), 'Part A: Summary of the report: Overall evaluation'; OfSTED, Burlington Junior School (inspection report), 'Part A: Summary of the report: Overall evaluation'.

3 In each maintained primary school OfSTED inspection report: 1) 'Part A: Summary of the report: Overall evaluation'. 2) 'Part D: Summary of the main inspection judgements: value for money provided by the school'.

4 OfSTED, Cheam Fields Primary School (inspection report), 'Leadership and management: Commentary'; OfSTED, Burlington Junior School (inspection report), 'Leadership and management: Commentary'.

5 Cited in the NUT response to OfSTED's consultation, *The Future of Inspection*: Shaw, I., Newton, D., Aitkin, M. and Darnell, R., 'Do OFSTED Inspections of Secondary Schools Make a Difference to GCSE Results?', *British Educational Research Journal*, Vol. 29, Mp/1, 2003. Rosenthal, L., *The Cost of Regulation in Education: Do School Inspections Improve School Quality?*, Keele: University of Keele, 2001.

6 OfSTED, *The Future of Inspection: Consultation Results*. (http://www.ofsted.gov.uk/howwework/index.cfm?fuseaction=howwework.future).

7 DfES, *A New Relationship with Schools: Improving Performance through Self-evaluation*, 2004.

8 OfSTED, Press notice: 'Radical new inspection arrangements will benefit parents, pupils and teachers', 9 March 2005.

9 OfSTED, *The Annual Report of Her Majesty's Chief Inspector of Schools 2004/05*, Commentary: David Bell, Her Majesty's Chief Inspector of Schools, October 2005.

10 OfSTED, *Strategic Plan 2005 to 2008*, November 2004.

11 House of Commons, 'Minutes of evidence taken before the Education and Skills Select Committee: the work of OfSTED: uncorrected transcript', November 2005.

12 OfSTED: Press notice: 'OfSTED announces five inspection providers to deliver new school inspection programme', 26 May 2005.

13 OfSTED, *The Annual Report of Her Majesty's Chief Inspector of Schools 2004/05*, conference speech, October 2005.

14 OfSTED, *Conducting the Inspection: Guidance for Inspectors: Inspecting Leadership and Management*, July 2005.

15 'OfSTED sets out expansion plans', *Guardian*, 9 May 2006.

16 Interview with unnamed teaching union representative, 23 January 2006.

17 National Audit Office, 'DfES: improving poorly performing schools in England', January 2006, cited in Marshall, P. *et al.*, *Aiming Higher: A Better Future for England's Schools*, Centre Forum, 2006.

18 Interview with Chris Woodhead, 3 February 2006.

19 OfSTED, *The Annual Report of Her Majesty's Chief Inspector of Schools 2004/05*.

20 National Union of Teachers, *The Response of the NUT to the OfSTED Consultation: The Future of Inspection*, 2004. (http://www.teachers.org.uk/resources/word/NUT_Rspns-Futue_of_Inspection.doc).

21 National Union of Teachers, *The Response of the NUT to the OfSTED Consultation: The Future of Inspection*, 2004. (http://www.teachers.org.uk/resources/word/NUT_Rspns-Futue_of_Inspection.doc).

22 National Association of Schoolmasters Union for Women Teachers (NASUWT), 'OfSTED's pronouncements increasingly irrelevant, says NASUWT', 25 January 2006.

23 National Association of Schoolmasters Union for Women Teachers (NASUWT), 2004.

24 'The Rockey road of inspection', *OfSTED Direct*, Issue 2, Spring Term 2004/05.

25 National Union of Teachers, *The Response of the NUT to the OfSTED Consultation: The Future of Inspection*, 2004. (http://www.teachers.org.uk/resources/word/NUT_Rspns-Futue_of_Inspection.doc).

26 OfSTED, Inspection reports for maintained primary school inspection from September 2005, 'Overall judgements'.

27 Macdonald, B., 'How education became nobody's business', in Altrichter, H. and Elliot, J. (eds), *Images of Education Change*, Buckingham: Open University, 2000, pp. 20-36, cited in The Australian Association for Research in Education, the association for active educational researchers, 2000, Smith, R., 'Quis custodiet ispsos custodies? Who will guard the guardians themselves?', An institutional evaluation of the New Zealand state's educational 'watchdog' agency: the Education Review Office (ERO)I UNITEC Institute of Technology, paper smi00320, 2000.

3: OfSTED in the Private Sector

1 Independent Schools Council, 2005-2006, *Snapshot: Independent Schooling in the United Kingdom*, 2005.

2 Interview with OfSTED inspector, 24 January 2006.

3 OfSTED, *Inspecting Independent Schools: The Framework for Inspecting Independent Schools in England under Section 162A of The Education Act 2002 in use from September 2005*, 'Introduction: the implications of the Education Act 2002', December 2005.

4 Department for Education and Skills, independent schools team, 11 May 2006.

5 OfSTED, *Inspecting Independent Schools: The Framework for Inspecting Independent Schools in England under Section 162A of The Education Act 2002 in use from September 2005*, 'Section 1: the basis for inspections: how often will schools be inspected?', December 2005.

6 Interview with OfSTED inspector, 24 January 2006.

7 OfSTED, *Inspection of Non-association Independent Schools*, July 2005.

8 Interview with OfSTED inspector, 24 January 2006.

9 Interview with OfSTED inspector, 24 January 2006.

10 Independent Schools Council, *Facts and Figures*, 'Numbers'. (http://www.isc.co.uk/index.php/5).

11 OfSTED, *Annual Report of Her Majesty's Chief Inspector of Schools 1996/1997*, 'Standards and quality in education: Independent schools', 1997.

12 OfSTED, *Annual Report of Her Majesty's Chief Inspector of Schools 1998/1999*, Standards and quality in education: Independent schools, 1999.

13 OfSTED, *Annual Report of Her Majesty's Chief Inspector of Schools 1998/1999*, Standards and quality in education: Independent schools, 1999.

14 Statutory Instruments: 2003 No.1910: Education, England, 'The Education (Independent School Standards) (England) Regulations 2003 as amended 17 January 2005'.

15 *Statutory Instruments: 2003 No.1910: Education, England*, 'The Education (Independent School Standards) (England) Regulations 2003 as amended 17 January 2005', 1: 3:g.

16 *Statutory Instruments: 2003 No. 1910: Education, England*, 'The Education (Independent School Standards) (England) Regulations 2003 as amended 17 January 2005', 1:3:c.

17 OfSTED, Cleve House School Inspection Report, 'Introduction and Summary: Next Steps', 2005.

18 Interview with OfSTED inspector, 24 January 2006.

19 OfSTED, Press release: 'Standards and inspections in independent schools'—David Bell HMCI: A talk at the Brighton College Conference on Independent Schools, 29 April 2003.

20 OfSTED, Press release: 'Standards and inspections in independent schools'—David Bell HMCI: A talk at the Brighton College Conference on Independent Schools, 29 April 2003.

21 OfSTED, *The Annual Report of Her Majesty's Chief Inspector of Schools 2004/05*, 'Overall effectiveness', 2005.

22 OfSTED, Press release: 'Standards and inspections in

independent schools', David Bell, HMCI: A talk at the Brighton College Conference on Independent Schools, 29 April 2003.

23 European Forum for Freedom in Education. (http://www.effe-eu.org/.)

24 Bell, R., European Forum for Freedom in Education, 'United Kingdom', London 2003.

25 Interview with Zoë Redhead, 23 January 2006.

26 Interview with Philip Bujak, Chief Executive of the Montessori Schools Association, 27 January 2006.

27 Interview with South School, 20 January 2006.

28 Interview with West School, 20 January 2006.

29 OfSTED, *Inspecting independent schools: The framework for inspecting independent schools in England under section 162A of The Education Act 2002 in use from September 2005*, 'Section 1: the basis for inspections: the principles governing inspections', December 2005.

30 General Secretary of an anonymous association in the Independent Schools Council, in interview, 20 January 2006.

31 Interview with OfSTED inspector, 24 January 2006.

32 Interview with East School, 31 January 2006.

33 Note: Roll numbers and school fees have been approximated in order to maintain the school's anonymity.

34 Interview with OfSTED inspector, 24 January 2006.

35 Interview with OfSTED inspector, 24 January 2006.

36 Interview with OfSTED inspector, 24 January 2006.

37 OfSTED, *About Us*, 'How we inspect independent schools'. (http://www.ofsted.gov.uk/howwework/index.cfm?fuseaction=howwework.inspections&id=5).

38 OfSTED, *How We Inspect Independent Schools*, 'What is an independent school inspection?'. http://www.ofsted.gov.uk/howwework/index.cfm?fuseaction=howwework.inspections&id=5).

39 Interview with association in the Independent Schools Council representative, 23 January 2006. Note: In the newly introduced 'second cycle' of inspections ISI reports have become shorter: this only reflects the fact that subjects are no longer looked at individually.

40 Interview with OfSTED inspector, 24 January 2006.

41 OfSTED, consultation on the framework for the inspection of independent schools, *Responses*, July 2003.

42 Interview sample: OfSTED, *South School* (inspection report), 'The quality of education provided by the school', 2005; OfSTED, *North School* (inspection report), 'The quality of education provided by the school', 2005; OfSTED, *East School* (inspection report), 'The quality of education provided by the school', 2005.

Report sample:

OfSTED, *Gower House School* (inspection report), 'The quality of education provided by the school', 2004. (http://www.ofsted.gov.uk/reports/manreports/1392.htm).

OfSTED, *Lyonsdown School* (inspection report), 'The quality of education provided by the school', 2004. (http://www.ofsted.gov.uk/reports/manreports/1522.htm).

OfSTED, *The Dower House School* (inspection report) 'The quality of education provided by the school', 2004. (http://www.ofsted.gov.uk/reports/manreports/1706.htm).

OfSTED, *Beehive Preparatory School* (inspection report), 'The quality of education provided by the school', 2004. (http://www.ofsted.gov.uk/reports/manreports/1631.htm).

43 OfSTED, *The Dower House School* (inspection report), 'The quality of education provided by the school', 2004; OfSTED, *Lyonsdown School* (inspection report), 'The quality of education provided by the school', 2004.

44 OfSTED, *Lyonsdown School* (inspection report), 'The quality of education provided by the school: the quality of the curriculum', 2004; OfSTED, *The Dower House School* (inspection report) 'The quality of education provided by the school: the quality of the curriculum', 2004; OfSTED, *Gower House School* (inspection report), 'The quality of education provided by the school: the quality of the curriculum', 2004; OfSTED, *Beehive Preparatory School* (inspection report), 'The quality of education provided by the school: the quality of the curriculum', 2004.

45 OfSTED, *Beehive Preparatory School* (inspection report), 'The quality of education provided by the school: the quality of the curriculum', 2004.

46 OfSTED, *Gower House School* (inspection report), 'The quality of education provided by the school: the quality of the curriculum', 2004.

47 DfES, *Independent Schools: Information Sheet.* (http://www.dfes.gov.uk/reg-independent-schools/Independent%20Schools%20Common%20Questions.doc).

48 OfSTED, Lyonsdown School (inspection report), 'The quality of education provided by the school: the quality of teaching and assessment', 2004; OfSTED, *The Dower House School* (inspection report) 'The quality of education provided by the school: the quality of teaching and assessment', 2004; OfSTED, *Gower House School* (inspection report), 'The quality of education provided by the school: the quality of teaching and assessment', 2004; OfSTED, *Beehive Preparatory School* (inspection report), 'The quality of education provided by the school: the quality of teaching and assessment', 2004.

49 OfSTED, *Lyonsdown School* (inspection report), 'The quality of education provided by the school: the quality of teaching and assessment', 2004; OfSTED, *The Dower House School* (inspection report) 'The quality of education provided by the school: the quality of teaching and assessment', 2004; OfSTED, *Gower House School* (inspection report), 'The quality of education provided by the school: the quality of teaching and assessment', 2004; OfSTED, *Beehive Preparatory School* (inspection report), 'The quality of education provided by the school: the quality of teaching and assessment', 2004.

50 OfSTED, *Lyonsdown School* (inspection report), 'The quality of education provided by the school: the quality of teaching and assessment', 2004; OfSTED, *Beehive Preparatory School* (inspection report) 'The quality of education provided by the school: the quality of teaching and assessment', 2004.

51 OfSTED, *Lyonsdown School* (inspection report), 'The quality of education provided by the school: the quality of teaching and assessment', 2004; OfSTED, *The Dower House School* (inspection report) 'The quality of education provided by the school: the quality of teaching and assessment', 2004; OfSTED, *Gower House School* (inspection report), 'The quality of education provided by the school: the quality of teaching and assessment', 2004; OfSTED, *Beehive Preparatory School* (inspection report), 'The

quality of education provided by the school: the quality of teaching and assessment', 2004.

52 OfSTED, *Gower House School* (inspection report), 'The quality of education provided by the school: the quality of teaching and assessment', 2004.

53 Report sample: OfSTED, *Lyonsdown School* (inspection report), 'Introduction and summary: summary of main findings', 2004; OfSTED, *The Dower House School* (inspection report), 'Introduction and summary: summary of main findings', 2004; OfSTED, *Gower House School* (inspection report), 'Introduction and summary: summary of main findings', 2004; OfSTED, *Beehive Preparatory School,* (inspection report) 'Introduction and summary: summary of main findings', 2004.

Interview sample: OfSTED, *South School* (inspection report), 'Introduction and summary: summary of main findings', 2005; OfSTED, *West School* (inspection report), 'Introduction and summary: summary of main findings', 2005; OfSTED, *East School* (inspection report), 'Introduction and summary: summary of main findings', 2005; OfSTED, *North School,* (inspection report), 'Introduction and summary: summary of main findings', 2005.

54 OfSTED, *The Dower House School* (inspection report), 'The quality of education provided by the school: the quality of teaching and assessment', 2004.

55 OfSTED, *The Dower House School* (inspection report), 'Summary of main findings', 2004.

56 OfSTED, *Annual Report of Her Majesty's Chief Inspector of Schools 1996/1997*, 'Standards and quality in education: Independent schools', 1997.

57 Interview with OfSTED inspector, 24 January 2006.

58 Interview with OfSTED inspector, 24 January 2006.

59 Report sample: OfSTED, *Gower House School* (inspection report), 'The quality of education provided by the school', 2004; OfSTED *The Dower House School* (inspection report), 'The quality of education provided by the school', 2004; OfSTED

Interview sample: OfSTED, *North School* (inspection report), 'The quality of education provided by the school', 2005.

60 Chevalier, A. and Dolton, P., 'The labour market for teachers' in Machin, S. and Vignoles, A. (eds), *What's the Good of Education?*

The Economics of Education in the UK, Princeton: Princeton University Press, 2005.

61 'Primary study attacks over-prescription', *Times Education Supplement,* 5 July 2002.

62 'Primary study attacks over-prescription', *Times Education Supplement,* 5 July 2002.

63 Interview with West School, 20 January 2006.

64 Chevalier, A. and Dolton, P., 'The labour market for teachers' in Machin, S. and Vignoles, A. (eds), *What's the Good of Education? The Economics of Education in the UK,* Princeton: Princeton University Press, 2005.

65 Interview with North school, 23 January 2006.

66 Report sample: OfSTED, *Gower House School* (inspection report), 'The quality of education provided by the school', 2004; OfSTED, *Lyonsdown School* (inspection report), 'The quality of education provided by the school: the quality of teaching and assessment', 2004.

Interview sample: OfSTED, *North School* (inspection report), 'The quality of education provided by the school: the quality of the teaching and assessment', 2005;

67 Interview with South School, 24 January 2006.

68 Interview with East School, 31 January 2006; interview with South School, 20 January 2006; interview with North School, 23 January 2006.

69 Report sample: OfSTED, *Lyonsdown School* (inspection report), 'The quality of education provided by the school: the quality of teaching and assessment', 2004; OfSTED, *The Dower House School* (inspection report), 'The quality of education provided by the school: the quality of teaching and assessment', 2004; OfSTED, *Beehive Preparatory School* (inspection report), 'The quality of education provided by the school: the quality of teaching and assessment', 2004.

Interview sample: OfSTED, *North School* (inspection report), 'The quality of education provided by the school: the quality of the teaching and assessment', 2005; OfSTED, *East School* (inspection report), 'The quality of education provided by the school: the quality of the teaching and assessment', 2005; OfSTED *South*

School (inspection report), 'The quality of education provided by the school: the quality of the teaching and assessment', 2005.

70 OfSTED, *The Dower House School* (inspection report), 'The quality of education provided by the school: the quality of teaching and assessment,' 2004.

71 OfSTED, *The Dower House School* (inspection report), 'The quality of education provided by the school: the quality of teaching and assessment,' 2004.

72 Report sample: OfSTED, *Gower House School* (inspection report), 'The quality of education provided by the school', 2004; OfSTED, *Lyonsdown School* (inspection report), 'The quality of education provided by the school: the quality of teaching and assessment', 2004; OfSTED, *Beehive Preparatory School* (inspection report), 'The quality of education provided by the school: the quality of teaching and assessment', 2004.

Interview sample: OfSTED, *North School* (inspection report), 'The quality of education provided by the school: the quality of the teaching and assessment', 2005; OfSTED, *South School* (inspection report), 'The quality of education provided by the school: the quality of the teaching and assessment', 2005; OfSTED, *West School* (inspection report), 'The quality of education provided by the school: the quality of the teaching and assessment', 2005.

73 OfSTED, *The Annual Report of Her Majesty's Chief Inspector of Schools, 2003/2004*, 'Independent schools', 2004.

74 John Bangs, 'Not too late for a strategic retreat', *Times Educational Supplement*, 16 May 2006; 'Goodbye computer chips', *Times Educational Supplement*, 19 May 2006.

75 *Statutory Instruments: 2003 No.1910: Education, England, The Education (Independent School Standards) (England) Regulations 2003 as amended 17 January 2005*, Premises and accommodation at schools; 5:a.

76 *Statutory Instruments: 2003 No.1910: Education, England, The Education (Independent School Standards) (England) Regulations 2003 as amended 17 January 2005*, Premises and accommodation at schools; 5:a.

77 Interview with South School, 20 January 2006.

78 Interview with West School, 20 January 2006; interview with South school, 20 January 2006.

79 OfSTED, *West School* (inspection report), 'The quality of education provided by the school: the quality of teaching assessment'.

80 Interview with West School, 20 January 2006.

81 South School inspection report, 'The quality of education provided by the school'; interview with South school, 20 January 2006.

82 Note: 'The Cognitive Abilities Test (CAT) is the most widely used test of reasoning ability in the UK. It measures the three principal areas of reasoning—verbal, non-verbal and numerical—as well as an element of spatial ability, allowing you to test the full range within an entire class or year'. (Taken from NFER/Nelson: http://www.nfer-nelson.co.uk/catalogue/catalogue_detail.asp?catid=84&id=1010).

83 OfSTED, *South School* (inspection report), inspection report, 'The quality of education provided by the school'; interview with South school, 20 January 2006.

84 Interview with West School, 20 January 2006.

85 OfSTED, *The Annual Report of Her Majesty's Chief Inspector of Schools 2004/05*, 'The quality of education and care: Independent schools: overall effectiveness', 2005.

86 OfSTED, *AboutUs*, 'How we inspect independent schools: what is an independent school inspection?'. (http://www.ofsted.gov.uk/howwework/index.cfm?fuseaction=howwework.inspections&id=5)

87 Head teacher of Gower House School in conversation, 24 April 2006.

88 OfSTED, *Beehive Preparatory School* (inspection report), 'The quality of education provided by the school', 2004.

89 Interview with Anthony Seldon, 28 January 2006.

90 Interview with North School, 23 January 2006.

91 Interview with South School, 20 January 2006.

92 Interview with West School, 20 January 2006.

93 Interview with South School, 20 January 2006.

94 OfSTED, *The Annual Report of Her Majesty's Chief Inspector of Schools 2004/05*, 'Commentary: David Bell, Her Majesty's Chief Inspector of Schools', October 2005.

4: Who Inspects the Inspectors?

1 Interview with anonymous association in the Independent Schools Council representative, 20 January 2006.

2 Interview with anonymous association in the Independent Schools Council representative, 20 January 2006.

3 Interview with Philip Bujak, Chief Executive of the Montessori Schools Association, 27 January 2006.

4 OfSTED, *Inspection of Non-association Independent Schools*, 'How long is an independent school inspection and what does it include?', July 2005. Note: ISI inspections have now been shortened by a day (interview with Head of Communications, Durell Barnes, ISI, 8 May 2006).

5 OfSTED, *Inspection of Non-association Independent Schools*, 'How long is an independent school inspection and what does it include?', July 2005.

6 Interview with West School, 20 January 2006.

7 Interview with anonymous association in the Independent Schools Council representative, 24 January 2006.

8 General Secretary of anonymous association in the Independent Schools Council, in interview, 20 January 2006.

9 Independent Schools Council, *Archive*, 'OfSTED emphasises its confidence in ISI', 25 November 2005.

10 ISI Information for parents. www.inspect.org.uk/geninfo/parents_230206_r.htm

11 Independent Schools Council, *Archive*, 'OfSTED emphasises its confidence in ISI', 25 November 2005.

12 Independent Schools Inspectorate, *December 2005 Bulletin*, 'From the Director, Tony Hubbard, to Inspectors and Schools', December 2005.

13 OfSTED: Independent Schools Council inspections 2003/04, November 2004.

14 OfSTED, *Independent Schools Council inspections 2003/04*, November 2004.

15 OfSTED, *Independent Schools Council inspections 2004/05*, November 2005.

16 OfSTED, *Independent Schools Council inspections 2003/04*, November 2004.

17 OfSTED, *Independent Schools Council inspections 2004/05*, November 2005.

18 Independent Schools Inspectorate, *December 2005 Bulletin*, 'From the Director, Tony Hubbard', 2005.

29 Independent Schools Inspectorate, *Archive*, 'OfSTED emphasises its confidence in ISI', 25 November 2005.

20 The United Kingdom Parliament, Private schools (Inspections): Dr Wright: 'Can it be right that there should be such a cosy complicity in the [independent school] inspection arrangements?' 21 February 2006.

21 Interview with anonymous association in the Independent Schools Council representative, 20 January 2006.

22 Independent Schools Inspectorate, *Information for Schools*, 'What is ISI?' (http://www.isinspect.org.uk/geninfo/Schools_info_0903_r.htm)

23 Independent Schools Council, *News*, 'ISC welcomes charities bill', 21 December 2004.

24 Independent Schools Council, *News*, 'ISC welcomes charities bill', 21 December 2004.

25 Independent Schools Council, *Facts and Figures*, 'Savings to the State'. (http.//www.isc.co.uk/index.php/5)

26 Independent Schools Council, *Facts and Figures*, 'Partnership'. (http://www.isc.co.uk/index.php/5).

27 'OfSTED to get tough on independents', *Guardian*, 29 April 2003.

28 'Top 50 independent schools found guilty of price-fixing to push up fees', *Guardian*, 10 November 2005.

29 'Private Schools Must Speak Out', *Independent*, 13 October 2005.

5: How Blair Became the School Bully

1 Spear, E.C., 'The Changing Pressure on Primary Schools' in Chitty, C. and Dunford, J. (eds), *State Schools: New Labour and the Conservative Legacy*, London: Woburn Press, 1999, p. 12.

2 Smithers, A., 'Education Policy' in Seldon, A. (ed.), *The Blair Effect*, London: Little Brown, 2001.

3 Tony Blair, speech: 'Our aim is a world class education system', September 2000 in Smithers, 'Education Policy', in *The Blair Effect*, 2001.

4 Hill, D., 'The Third Way in Britain: New Labour's neo-liberal education policy', paper presented at Congres Marx International III, Universite de Paris-X Nanterre-Sorbonne, September 2001.

5 Tony Halpin, 'Analysis: Primary school tests', *The Times*, 23 August 2005.

6 Steve Sinnott, general secretary of the NUT quoted in the *Guardian*, 'Tests show gender gap widening at primary school', 24 August 2005.

7 Smithers, 'Education Policy' in *The Blair Effect*, 2001.

8 Tony Halpin, 'Analysis: Primary school tests', *The Times*, 23 August 2005.

9 Smithers, 'Education Policy' in *The Blair Effect*, 2001.

10 Tony Halpin, 'Results improve but doubts linger over their value', *The Times*, 2 December 2005.

11 BBC News Online, 'Top heads say scrap school tables', 2 December 2005.

12 Jacqui Smith, Minister for Schools Standards, in Tony Halpin, 'Results improve but doubts linger over their value', *The Times*, 2 December 2005.

13 'Key Stage 2 English pass mark was set too low, low three-year study finally reveals', *Times Educational Supplement*, 19 December 2003.

14 Interview with Peter Tymms, director of CEM, 27 January 2006.

15 Curriculum Evaluation and Management Centre (CEM), University of Durham: Performance Indicators in Primary Schools (PIPS) Project: Standards over Time, 2002. www.pipsproject.org/standardsovertime.asp

16 'Primary school improvement exaggerated', *Guardian*, 23 August 2006.

17 'Targets', *Daily Mail*, 19 September 2003.

18 'Schools are blamed for lacklustre approach to reading', *The Times*, 15 December 2004.

19 Tony Halpin, 'Primary schools report: results improve but doubts linger over their value', *The Times*, 2 December 2005.

20 *Times Educational Supplement*, 11 June 2004.

21 Interview with Peter Tymms, 27 January 2006.

22 Alexander, R., *Culture and Pedagogy: International Comparisons in Primary Education*, Oxford: Blackwell, 2000, cited in Brown, M., Askew, M., Baker, D., Denvir, H., and Millett, A. 'Is the National Numeracy Strategy research-based?' *British Journal of Educational Studies*, 46 (4), pp. 362-385. Hughes, M., 'The National Numeracy Strategy: are we getting it right?', *Psychology of Education Review*, 23(2), 1999, pp. 3-7.

23 Brown, Askew, Baker, Denvir and Millett, 'Is the National Numeracy Strategy research-based?' *British Journal of Educational Studies*, 46 (4), pp. 362-385.

24 'Is the literacy hour damaging young children's ability to speak and think?', *Times Educational Supplement*, 3 May 2002.

25 'Is the Literacy hour damaging young children's ability to speak and think?', *Times Educational Supplement*, 3 May 2002; (original journal article) Hargreaves, L. and Moyles, J., Merry, R. Paterson, ASF and Esarte-Sarries, V., 'How do elementary school teachers define and implement interactive teaching in the national literacy hour in England?', presented at the American Educational Research Association Conference, New Orleans, 2002.

26 Docking, J., 'Curriculum Initiatives,' in Docking, J., (ed.) *New Labour's Policies for Schools: Raising the Standard?*, London: David Fulton Publishers, 2000, p. 71.

27 'Tories launch assault on "red tape"', *Guardian*, 7 July 2004.

28 BBC News Online, 'Head to head: Schools White Paper', 5 February 2006.

29 Chevalier, A. and Dolton, P., 'The labour market for teachers' in Machin, S. and Vignoles, A. (eds), *What's the Good of Education? The Economics of Education in the UK* Princeton: Princeton University Press, 2005.

30 Smithers, A. and Robinson, P., 'Factors affecting teachers' decisions to leave the profession', *DfES Research Report*, 430, 2003.

31 Cited in Marshall, P., Moses, J. and Seed, E., *Aiming Higher: A Better Future for England's Schools*, London: Centre Forum, 2006.

32 Cited in Marshall, P., Moses, J., and Seed, E., *Aiming Higher: A Better Future for England's Schools*, London: Centre Forum, 2006.

33 Politics.co.uk, 'Mixed results for Labour on education', 9 May 2005. Note: Study commissioned by the Association of Teachers and Lecturers, 2005.

34 Anthony Seldon, 'Partnerships will reduce the schools chasm', *Times Educational Supplement*, 17 February 2006.

35 Di Maggio, P.J. and Powell, W., 'The iron cage revisited: institutional isomorphism and collective rationality in organizational fields' in Calhoun, C. *et al.* (eds), *Contemporary Sociological Theory*, Oxford: Blackwell Publishing, 2002.

36 Flynn, N., *Public Sector Management*, Hemel Hempstead: Harvester Wheatsheaf, 1990; Walsh, K., *Public Services and Market Mechanisms: Competition, Contracting and the New Public Management*, Basingstoke: Macmillan, 1995, cited in Clarke, J. and Newman, J., *The Managerial State: Power, Politics and Ideology in the Remaking of Social Welfare*, London: Sage, 1997.

37 Clarke and Newman, *The Managerial State: Power, Politics and Ideology in the Remaking of Social Welfare*, 1997, p. 33.

38 Peters, T. and Waterman, R., *In Search of Excellence: Lessons from America's Best-run Companies*, New York: Harper and Row, 1982, cited in Clarke and Newman, *The Managerial State: Power, Politics and Ideology in the Remaking of Social Welfare*, 1997.

39 Coffey, A., *Education and Social Change*, Buckingham: Open University Press, 2001.

40 Wilmott, R., *Education Policy and Realist Social Theory*, London: Routledge, 2002.

41 Chitty, C., 'Central Control of the School Curriculum 1944 -1986' in Moon, B. (ed.), *New Curriculum-National Curriculum*, Milton Keynes: Hodder and Stoughton, 1990.

42 Smyth and Shacklock quoted in Ball, S., 'Performativity and Fragmentation in "Postmodern Schooling"' in Carter, J. (ed.), *Postmodernity and the Fragmentation of Welfare*, London: Routledge, 1998.

43 Wilmott, R., *Education Policy and Realist Social Theory*,London: Routledge, 2002.

44 Ferguson, R., 'Modernizing managerialism: the case of

education', in Clarke, J., Gewirtz, S. and McLaughlin, E. (eds), *New Managerialism, New Welfare?* London: Sage, 2000.

45 Gewirtz, S., Centre for Public Policy Research, King's College London, 'Achieving Success? Critical reflections on New Labour's 'third way' agenda for education', Keynote Lecture to International Meeting on Curriculum Politics, Oporto, May 2002.

46 Gewirtz, 'Achieving Success? Critical reflections on New Labour's 'third way' agenda for education', Keynote Lecture to International Meeting on Curriculum Politics, Oporto, May 2002.

47 Wilmott, R., *Education Policy and Realist Social Theory*, London: Routledge, 2002.

48 Di Maggio, P.J. and Powell, W., 'The iron cage revisited: institutional isomorphism and collective rationality in organizational fields' in Calhoun, C. *et al.* (eds), *Contemporary Sociological Theory*, Oxford: Blackwell Publishing, 2002.

49 Hartley, D., *Re-schooling Society*, London: The Falmer Press, *1997;* Shore, C.and Wright, S., 'Audit Culture and Anthropology: Neo-liberalism in British Higher Education' in *The Journal of the Royal Anthropological Institute: Incorporating Man*, Vol. 5, No. 4, 1999.

50 Hoggett, P., quoted in Clarke and Newman, *The Managerial State: Power, Politics and Ideology in the Remaking of Social Welfare*, 1997, p. 13.

51 Navarro, V., 'Is there a third way? A response to Giddens's the third way', *International Journal of Health Sciences*, 29 (4), pp. 667-677, quoted in Gewirtz, 'Achieving Success? Critical reflections on New Labour's 'third way' agenda for education', Keynote Lecture to International Meeting on Curriculum Politics, Oporto, May 2002.

52 Giddens, A., *The Third Way: The Renewal of Social Democracy*, Cambridge, Polity Press, 1998, p. 99.

53 Giddens, *The Third Way: The Renewal of Social Democracy*, 1998.

54 Giddens, *The Third Way: The Renewal of Social Democracy*, 1998, p. 74.

55 Giddens, *The Third Way: The Renewal of Social Democracy*, 1998.

56 Michael Howard QC MP, Speech to the Heads Conference of the National Grammar Schools Association, 17 June 2004, cited in

O'Shaughnessy, J. and Leslie, C., *More Good School Places*, London: Policy Exchange, 2005.

57 Weber, M., *Economy and Society: An Outline of Interpretive Sociology*, Berkeley: University of California Press, 1978, p. 957.

58 Mouzelis, N.P., *Organization and Bureaucracy: An Analysis of Modern Theories*, London: Routledge and Kegan Paul, 1975, p. 59.

59 Marr, A., *Ruling Britannia: The Failure and Future of British Democracy*, London: Michael Joseph, 1995.

60 Gewirtz, 'Achieving Success? Critical reflections on New Labour's 'third way' agenda for education', Keynote Lecture to International Meeting on Curriculum Politics, Oporto, May 2002.

61 Rose, N., 'Governing "advanced" liberal democracies' in Barry, A., Osborne, T. and Rose, N. (eds), *Foucault and Political Reason: Liberalism, Neo-liberalism and Rationalities of Government*, London: University College London Press, 2001, p. 12.

62 Clarke J. and Newman, J., *The Managerial State: Power, Politics and Ideology in the Remaking of Social Welfare*, London: Sage, 1997.

63 Weber, M., *Economy and Society: An Outline of Interpretive Sociology*, Berkeley: University of California Press, 1978.

64 Giddens, A., *Sociology*, 2nd edn, Cambridge: Polity Press, 1994.

65 Weber, *Economy and Society: An Outline of Interpretive Sociology*, 1978, cited in Giddens, *Sociology*, 2nd edn, 1994.

66 Labour Party manifesto 2005, Education.

67 Hill, D., 'The Third Way in Britain: New Labour's neo-liberal education policy', paper presented at Congres Marx International III, Universite de Paris-X Nanterre-Sorbonne, September 2001.

68 Chevalier, A. and Dolton, P., 'The labour market for teachers' in Machin, S. and Vignoles, A. (eds), *What's the Good of Education? The Economics of Education in the UK*, Princeton: Princeton University Press, 2005.

69 Letters, *Times Educational Supplement*, 27 January 2006.

70 Tony Blair, 'White Paper a "pivotal" moment for schooling', speech at 10 Downing Street, 24 October 2005.

71 'Teacher Training Quality is the Best Ever', *Times Educational Supplement*, 20 June 2003.

72 Coffey, A., *Education and Social Change*, Buckingham Open University Press, 2001, p. 2.

73 *Times Educational Supplement*, 28 April 2006.

74 Chevalier and Dolton, 'The labour market for teachers' in *What's the Good of Education? The Economics of Education in the UK*, 2005.

75 Di Maggio and Powell, 'The iron cage revisited: institutional isomorphism and collective rationality in organizational fields' in *Contemporary Sociological Theory*, 2002.

76 Power, M., 'The audit society' in Hopwood, A.G. and Miller, P., *Accounting as Social and Institutional Practice*, Cambridge: Cambridge University Press, 1994, p. 301.

77 Armstrong, P. in Power, 'The audit society' in *Accounting as Social and Institutional Practice*, 1994.

78 Power, 'The Audit Society' in *Accounting as Social and Institutional Practice*, 1994.

79 Rose, 'Governing "advanced" liberal democracies', in *Foucault and Political Reason: Liberalism, Neo-liberalism and Rationalities of Government*, 2001.

80 Power, 'The Audit Society' in *Accounting as Social and Institutional Practice*, 1994.

81 Gudeman, S., 'The New Captains of Information' in *Journal of the Royal Anthropological Institute: Incorporating Man*, Vol. 14, No. 1, 1998, cited in Shore, C. and Wright, S., 'Audit Culture and Anthropology: Neo-liberalism in British Higher Education' in *The Journal of the Royal Anthropological Institute: Incorporating Man*, Vol. 5, No. 4, 1999.

82 Strathern, M., *Audit Cultures: Anthropological Studies in Accountability, Ethics and the Academy*, London: Routledge, 2000, cited in Shore and Wright, 'Audit Culture and Anthropology: Neo-liberalism in British Higher Education' in *The Journal of the Royal Anthropological Institute: Incorporating Man*, 1999.

83 Shore and Wright, 'Audit Culture and Anthropology: Neo-liberalism in British Higher Education' in *The Journal of the Royal Anthropological Institute: Incorporating Man*, Vol. 5, No. 4, 1999.

84 Foucault, M., *Discipline and Punish: The Birth of the Prison*, London: Penguin, 1991.

85 OfSTED, *The Annual Report of Her Majesty's Chief Inspector of Schools*

2004/05, Commentary: David Bell, Her Majesty's Chief Inspector of Schools, October 2005.

86 Interview with anonymous teaching union representative, 20 January 2006.

87 Martin, L.H., Gutman H. and Hutton, P.H., *Technologies of the Self: A seminar with Michel Foucault*, Massachusetts, University of Massachusetts Press, 1988.

88 OfSTED, *School inspections*, 'Changes to OfSTED inspections from September 2005', 2005.

89 OfSTED, 'Standards and inspections in independent schools'—David Bell HMCI: A talk at the Brighton College Conference Independent Schools, 29 April 2003.

90 O'Neill, O., 'Trust and Transparency', Reith Lecture, 2002.

91 Beck, U., *The Reinvention of Politics: Rethinking Modernity in the Global Social Order*, Cambridge: Polity Press, 1999.

92 Ball, S.J., 'Performativities and fabrications in the education economy: towards the performative society' in Ball, S.J. (ed.), The RoutledgeFalmer *Reader in Sociology of Education*, London: Routledge Falmer, 2004, p. 146.

93 Ball, 'Performativities and fabrications in the education economy: towards the performative society' in *Reader in Sociology of Education*, 2004, p. 148.

94 Ball, 'Performativities and fabrications in the education economy: towards the performative society' in *Reader in Sociology of Education*, 2004, p. 150

95 Power, 'The audit society' in *Accounting as Social and Institutional Practice*, 1994.

6: Conclusion

1 Independent School Council, *Statistical Survey of Independent Schools Council*, January 2004.

2 Reference to Charles Clarke, then Secretary of State for Education, *The Socialist*, 14-20 April 2005.

3 Tessa Keswick, Centre for Policy Studies commission for the *Sunday Telegraph*, 'Did things *only* get better?', *Sunday Telegraph*, 3 June 2001.

4 OECD, *Education at a Glance 2004: OECD Indicators*, 'The learning environment and organisation of schools, class size and ratio of students to teaching staff'.

5 Labour Party manifesto 1997, Education.

6 Smithers, A. and Robinson, P., *Teachers Leaving*, Centre for Education and Employment, 18 December 2002.

7 National Audit Office: 'DfES: improving poorly performing schools in England', January 2006.

8 The United Kingdom Parliament, House of Lords, Hansard text for 11 January 2005, column 240.

9 'State school told it cannot complain about OfSTED', *Daily Telegraph*, 6 December 2005.

10 OfSTED: 'The future of inspection: consultation results'. (http://www.ofsted.gov.uk/howwework/index.cfm?fuseaction =howwework.future).

11 Lord Skidelsky, 1997, paraphrased in Docking, J., 'What is the solution? An overview of national policies for schools, 1979-99' in Docking J. (ed.), *New Labour's Policies for Schools: Raising the Standard?*, London: David Fulton Publishers Ltd, 2000, p. 40.

Appendix 1: Charterhouse Square School

1 OfSTED, *Charterhouse Square School* (inspection report), 'Information about the school', 2004. (http://www.ofsted.gov.uk/reports/manreports/1582.htm)

2 Charterhouse Square School website: www.thecharterhousesesquareschool.co.uk

3 OfSTED, *Inspecting independent schools: The framework for inspecting independent schools in England under section 162A of The Education Act 2002 in use form September 2005*, 'Section 1: the basis for inspections: how often will schools be inspected?', December 2005.

4 OfSTED, *How We Inspect Independent Schools*, 'What are the results of an independent school inspection?' (http://www.ofsted.gov.uk/howwework/index.cfm?fuseaction =howwework.inspections&id=5)

5 OfSTED, *Charterhouse Square School* (inspection report), 'Summary of main findings', 2004.

6 OfSTED, *Charterhouse Square School* (inspection report), 'The quality of education provided by the school: the quality of the curriculum', 2004.

7 OfSTED, *Charterhouse Square School* (inspection report), 'The quality of education provided by the school: the quality of the curriculum', 2004.

8 OfSTED, *Charterhouse Square School* (inspection report), 'The quality of education provided by the school: the quality of the curriculum', 2004.

9 OfSTED, *Charterhouse Square School* (inspection report), 'The quality of education provided by the school: the quality of the curriculum', 2004.

10 OfSTED, *Charterhouse Square School* (inspection report), 'The quality of education provided by the school: the quality of the curriculum', 2004.

11 OfSTED, *Charterhouse Square School* (inspection report), 'The quality of education provided by the school: the quality of the curriculum', 2004.

12 OfSTED, *Charterhouse Square School* (inspection report), 'The quality of education provided by the school: the quality of the curriculum', 2004.

13 OfSTED, *Charterhouse Square School* (inspection report), 'The quality of education provided by the school: the quality of the curriculum', 2004.

14 OfSTED, *Charterhouse Square School* (inspection report), 'The quality of education provided by the school: the quality of the curriculum', 2004.

15 OfSTED, *Charterhouse Square School* (inspection report), 'The quality of education provided by the school: the quality of the curriculum', 2004.

16 OfSTED, *Charterhouse Square School* (inspection report), 'The quality of education provided by the school: the quality of the teaching and assessment, 2004.

17 OfSTED, *Charterhouse Square School* (inspection report), 'The quality of education provided by the school: the quality of the teaching and assessment, 2004.

18 OfSTED, *Charterhouse Square School* (inspection report), 'The quality of education provided by the school: the quality of the teaching and assessment, 2004.

19 OfSTED, *Charterhouse Square School* (inspection report), 'The quality of education provided by the school: the quality of the teaching and assessment, 2004.

20 OfSTED, *Charterhouse Square School* (inspection report), 'The quality of education provided by the school: the quality of the teaching and assessment, 2004.

21 OfSTED, *Charterhouse Square School* (inspection report), 'The quality of education provided by the school: the quality of teaching and assessment, 2004.

22 OfSTED, *Charterhouse Square School* (inspection report), 'The quality of education provided by the school: the quality of the curriculum', 2004.

23 OfSTED, *Charterhouse Square School* (inspection report), 'The quality of education provided by the school: the quality of the curriculum', 2004.

24 OfSTED, *Charterhouse Square School* (inspection report), 'The welfare, health and safety of the pupils', 2004.

25 OfSTED, *Charterhouse Square School* (inspection report), 'The suitability of the proprietor and staff', 2004.

26 OfSTED, *Charterhouse Square School* (inspection report), 'The suitability of the premises and accommodation', 2004.

Appendix 2: Two Case Studies

1 HMCI David Bell, OfSTED, *Annual Report 2004/2005*, October 2005.

2 OECD, 'Teachers matter: attracting, developing and retaining effective teachers', June 2005, cited in Marshall, P., Moses, J. and Seed, E., *Aiming Higher: A Better Future for England's Schools*, London: Centre Forum, 2006.